Advanced Filter Structure Handbook

Haipeng Dai • Meng Li • Guihai Chen

Advanced Filter Structure Handbook

From Design to Optimization

Springer

Haipeng Dai
School of Computer Science
Nanjing University
Nanjing, Jiangsu, China

Meng Li
School of Computer Science
Nanjing University
Nanjing, Jiangsu, China

Guihai Chen
School of Computer Science
Nanjing University
Nanjing, Jiangsu, China

ISBN 978-981-95-1714-5 ISBN 978-981-95-1715-2 (eBook)
https://doi.org/10.1007/978-981-95-1715-2

This Springer imprint is published by the registered company Springer Nature Singapore Pte Ltd.
The registered company address is: 152 Beach Road, #21-01/04 Gateway East, Singapore 189721, Singapore

Preface

Filters are compact probabilistic data structures widely used for membership testing, i.e., determining whether an element belongs to a given set. Commonly, they have a one-sided error property: they definitely report yes if the query element belongs to the set; however, they have a certain probability to falsely report yes for elements not present in the set. By compactly representing elements with only a few bits per item, they achieve low memory overhead and high space efficiency. As a result, filters have become indispensable across diverse domains for efficient data querying.

This book focuses on four major classes of filter data structures: read-only filters optimized for static or slowly changing datasets, space-resilient filters designed to withstand memory constraints or errors, streaming filters for dynamic data streams, and range filters supporting multi-dimensional or interval-based membership queries. These four filter categories stems from their collective capacity to comprehensively address the core challenges and diverse use cases in modern data filtering systems.

We assume that the reader is familiar with basic data structures such as arrays, linked lists, queues, stacks, binary trees, and hash tables, typically covered in fundamental data structures and algorithms courses. We also expect some knowledge of computer organization, storage structures, and a basic understanding of LSM-trees and database systems. The filters discussed in this book build on these data structures to create more complex designs common in database systems. Since the book focuses on advanced filter structures, prior knowledge of basic filters such as Bloom and cuckoo filters will be helpful.

Nanjing, China
July 2025

Haipeng Dai
Meng Li
Guihai Chen

Acknowledgments This work was partially supported by the National Key R&D Program of China (Grant No. 2023YFB4502400) and the National Natural Science Foundation of China (62272223 and 62422207). Besides, we would like to thank Huayi Chai, Zhaochen Zhou, Zhipeng Chen, Shusen Chen, Yunchuan Liu, Xuequ Huang, Zhihan Jiang, and Shizhe Liu for the assistance.

Contents

Chapter 1
Introduction

Abstract Filters are essential probabilistic data structures used for membership testing, efficiently determining if an element belongs to a set. They offer low memory overhead and high throughput by representing elements compactly, often residing in CPU caches. As a result, filters have become indispensable across diverse domains for efficient data querying. This chapter introduces the fundamental concept of filters, application scenarios, and four categories of filters designed for varying scenarios.

Keywords Filters · Membership testing · High-performance query

1.1 Filter Structures Are Foundational

Filters are compact probabilistic data structures widely used for membership testing, i.e., determining whether an element belongs to a given set. Commonly, they have a one-sided error property: they definitely report yes if the query element belongs to the set; however, they have a certain probability to falsely report yes for elements not present in the set. By compactly representing elements with only a few bits per item, they achieve low memory overhead and high space efficiency. As a result, filters can reside in CPU L1/L2 cache, thereby enabling high insertion and query throughput. Generally, filters contain three components: (1) a bit array to encode an element set, (2) multiple hash functions or probabilistic encoding schemes to map elements into the bit array, and (3) some key operation algorithms, e.g., insertion, membership checking, deletion, and update (note that the last two operations are not vital in some cases). Prevalent filters include Bloom filter (BF), Xor filter, Cuckoo filter (CF), Quotient filter, and their variants. Each of them is tailored to specific trade-offs between space, accuracy, and operational flexibility.

Figure 1.1 illustrates the structure of Bloom filter (BF). Initially, BF first creates a bit array and sets all bits to 0. When inserting an element into the element set, BF uses k independent hash functions $h_1(\cdot), ..., h_k(\cdot)$ obeying uniform distribution to map the element to k bits in the array and set them to 1. For checking whether

H. Dai et al., *Advanced Filter Structure Handbook*,
https://doi.org/10.1007/978-981-95-1715-2_1

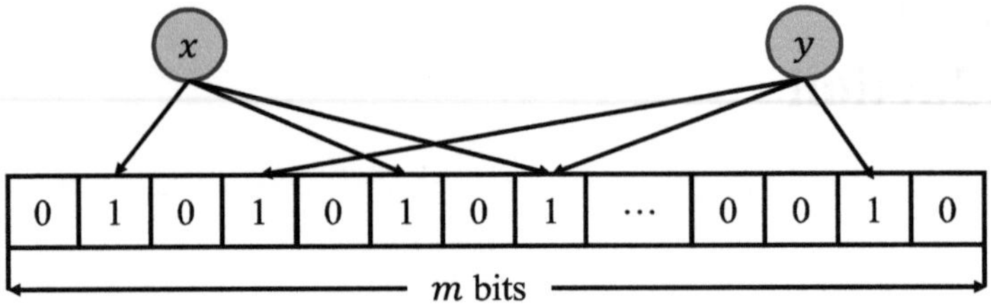

Fig. 1.1 Example of a standard Bloom filter

an element belongs to S, BF reports yes if all k mapped bits of the item are 1. Otherwise, BF reports no, which means this element does not belong to the set.

Since filters provide one-sided error guarantees, low space overhead, and high insertion and query throughput, filters have become indispensable across diverse domains for efficient data querying. Several key applications include the following: (1) In key-value store systems, filters like Bloom filters and Cuckoo indexes are incorporated into LSM-tree indexes to significantly reduce unnecessary disk I/O during queries, greatly enhancing performance. (2) In network routing, filters enable rapid lookups for blocked IPs/domains in firewalls, cutting packet processing latency while using minimal memory. (3) In real-time applications, such as fraud detection and analytics, filters effectively track membership in unbounded data streams with nearly constant memory usage. (4) In distributed systems, space-resilient filters replicate membership information across nodes with low synchronization costs, and range filters expedite interval queries in time-series databases and geospatial systems.

The importance of filter data structures has grown exponentially with the proliferation of big data and edge computing. As applications increasingly deal with data volumes that exceed available memory or traverse slow I/O channels, filters serve as lightweight gatekeepers, reducing unnecessary data movement and computation. For example, in cloud storage systems, read-only filters can reject up to 90% of invalid key lookups before accessing slower disk storage, while space-resilient filters allow IoT devices with constrained memory to maintain approximate membership states despite hardware limitations. Moreover, as hardware evolves—with the rise of nonvolatile memory, parallel processing architectures, and energy-efficient chips—the design of filters must adapt to leverage new storage hierarchies and computational paradigms, driving continuous innovation in the field.

This book focuses on four major classes of filter data structures: read-only filters optimized for static or slowly changing datasets, space-resilient filters designed to withstand memory constraints or errors, streaming filters for dynamic data streams, and range filters supporting multidimensional or interval-based membership queries.

The rationale for focusing on these four filter categories stems from their collective capacity to comprehensively address the core challenges and diverse use cases in modern data filtering systems. These classes were not arbitrarily selected; rather, they embody fundamental dimensions that structure advanced filtering requirements: operational modality, resource constraint tolerance, data processing paradigm, and query semantics. Indeed, these four dimensions form an interconnected core rather than isolated criteria, defining the very essence of filter design challenges. Operational modality establishes the foundational interaction between data structures and workloads, determining whether a filter prioritizes read efficiency for static datasets or adaptability for dynamic updates. Resource constraint tolerance, in turn, serves as a critical modifier, shaping how operational strategies must evolve under memory or power limitations—consider how a space–resilient filter adapts the read-only paradigm to constrained environments. Data processing paradigm introduces a temporal dimension, compelling filters to align with either batch-style static analysis or real-time streaming requirements, which in turn influences the expression of query semantics: a streaming filter's continuous data ingestion demands query models capable of handling evolving membership states, while range filters rely on structured query semantics to leverage ordered data domains.

Specifically, (1) read-only filters establish the foundational operational framework by defining how static data structures interact with read-heavy workloads, serving as the baseline against which more dynamic filter behaviors are measured; (2) space-resilient filters extend this foundation by addressing the critical challenge of memory efficiency in resource-constrained environments, a dimension increasingly important as applications migrate to edge computing and low-power devices; (3) streaming filters then shift the focus to temporal data dynamics, handling continuous data inflows that characterize modern IoT, financial trading, and real-time analytics systems; and (4) range filters specialize in semantic query complexity, enabling nuanced data retrieval across ordered domains that are essential for database indexing, scientific computing, and geospatial applications. Together, they form a design matrix that captures the essential trade-offs in filter design—between space and time efficiency, static vs. dynamic data environments, simple vs. complex query logic, and resource-rich vs. resource-constrained deployments. By focusing on these four archetypes, practitioners gain a holistic toolkit: read-only filters provide foundational correctness guarantees, space-resilient filters ensure deployability in harsh environments, streaming filters enable real-time decision-making, and range filters unlock analytical depth. This combination neither overcomplicates with redundant special cases nor underserves by missing critical use cases, making it the ideal framework for navigating the advanced filter design space.

By dissecting their design principles, performance trade-offs, and real-world use cases, the book aims to equip readers with the knowledge to (1) select the right filter for a given workload, such as balancing false positive rates (FPRs) against update frequency, (2) adapt existing filters to emerging hardware or data patterns, and (3) design novel filter variants for unmet challenges in areas like privacy-preserving computation or high-frequency trading. As data-intensive applications continue to push the boundaries of scale and speed, mastering filter data structures has become essential for building efficient, scalable, and resilient systems.

1.2 Trade-Offs in Filter Structure Design

Filters, despite their varying design principles, share certain commonalities and trade-offs. Key considerations in filter design include occupied space, false positive rate (FPR), construction, and query time complexity, as well as the algorithm's effectiveness. Some factors conflict and typically cannot be optimized simultaneously. For example, a low FPR needs a larger space allocation for filters. From a system perspective, the core goal of filters is to utilize efficient algorithms to minimize the time complexity of filter construction and queries while maintaining acceptable FPR and space usage.

1.2.1 Read-Only Filters Design

Read-only filters are commonly employed in LSM-tree-based storage systems to facilitate efficient point queries. In such systems, the default filter implementation is BF. Although BF enables efficient existence testing for query data, it suffers from two inherent limitations: (1) their space overhead significantly exceeds the information-theoretic lower bound and (2) queries require multiple random memory accesses, resulting in poor locality.

To address these issues, several alternative filters have been proposed, with three primary optimizations emerging. First, Xor filters store fingerprints via XOR operations in a compact array, and they use only three hash functions rather than k. Compared with Bloom filters, Xor filters achieve higher query throughput and lower false positive rates (FPRs). Second, ribbon filters build upon Xor filters by introducing sparse matrix algebra; they further optimize space efficiency and reduce memory accesses through linear equation solving. Third, binary fuse filters enhance Xor filters via two-tiered hashing and binary search. They attain near-optimal space utilization approaching the information-theoretic limit and maintain constant-time queries with just two memory accesses.

Read-only filters consume compact memory spaces and process queries with low latency, making them particularly suitable for SSTable (Sorted String Table) filter blocks in LSM-tree storage engines, read-only caching systems, resource-constrained embedded devices, and edge computing infrastructures with limited memory bandwidth.

1.2.2 Space-Resilient Filters Design

Traditional filter data structures, such as BF, have been extensively applied in domains like caching and data deduplication, primarily due to their high space utilization efficiency and excellent query performance. However, they still exhibit significant limitations. Before employing a BF, the quantity of data to be inserted must be determined in advance so as to allocate a fixed-size space. Once the amount of inserted data surpasses the preset upper limit of the space's capacity, its FPR will surge substantially. This, in turn, leads to a notable decline in the accuracy of the filtering results, rendering it unable to meet the requirements in scenarios where the data volume changes dynamically.

Space-resilient filters, a category of filter data structures that support dynamic capacity expansion and contraction, possess a core advantage: they can flexibly adjust their internal structures in response to fluctuations in data volume. In contrast to traditional fixed-capacity filters, such as BF, space-resilient filters are not constrained by predefining the data volume. When the amount of data to be inserted increases, these filters can automatically expand their storage space, thereby preventing a sharp increase in the false positive rate caused by insufficient space. Conversely, when the data volume decreases, they are capable of shrinking the space, releasing redundant resources, and enhancing the space utilization efficiency.

1.2.3 Streaming Filters Design

In the era of explosive data growth, data within data stream application scenarios exhibits characteristics of being unbounded and in continuous flow. The data volume is enormous, and its growth rate is extremely rapid.

Traditional deduplication techniques encounter significant challenges when handling such data streams. Owing to the unbounded nature of data streams, accurately eliminating duplicate data would require nearly infinite storage space, which is practically unfeasible in real-world applications. Take the traditional bloom filter as an illustration. Despite its ability to efficiently determine the existence of an element when dealing with a limited amount of data, due to its fixed storage space constraints, it struggles to accommodate the constantly incoming unbounded data streams. Once the data volume surpasses its capacity, the misjudgment rate will soar dramatically, failing to meet the requirements for processing duplicate data in data stream applications.

Against this backdrop, the streaming filters have emerged. Specifically designed for unbounded data stream environments, it is capable of roughly eliminating duplicate data within a given limited space. By leveraging innovative data structures and algorithms, the streaming filters effectively reduce memory usage while adapting to the continuous and rapid nature of data streams. This significantly enhances the efficiency and feasibility of duplicate data processing in data stream applications, providing robust support for the real-time analysis and processing of data streams. As a result, it has become an essential and pivotal technology in modern data stream applications.

1.2.4 Range Filters Design

In many database systems, storage systems, and applications, range queries are widely employed in numerous scenarios. Most of the aforementioned filters can only support point queries. To utilize them for range queries, one must convert the range query into multiple individual point queries covering the target interval, which leads to higher time complexity. In some cases, range queries may not even be able to convert to point queries. Consequently, range filters have emerged as a solution since they are capable of processing range queries with low time complexity while maintaining the precision of point queries.

Range filters are typically employed in LSM-tree-based storage systems as the content of filter blocks within SSTables (Sorted String Tables) to facilitate both point queries and range queries. After construction, range filters generally occupy a small memory space, allowing them to reside persistently in memory. Similar to other probabilistic filters, range filters exhibit one-sided error properties (i.e., they may yield false positives but never false negatives). During query execution, the system first probes the in-memory range filter. If the filter determines that the target key does not exist, the system can avoid loading the corresponding SSTable into memory, thereby significantly improving query efficiency.

Range filters can be broadly categorized into four types based on their construction methods; they are prefix-based, hash-based, learning-based, and hybrid. Prefix-based range filters typically employ data structures such as binary trees or prefix trees (tries), optimizing performance for large-range queries. Hash-based range filters utilize techniques like layered bloom filters or piecewise monotonically increasing hash functions, making them efficient for small-range queries. Notably, hash-based range filters that apply hash operations to key suffixes enhance the robustness of the filter. Learning-based range filters leverage linear regression models (or other machine learning techniques) to approximate the distribution of the underlying dataset. These filters are characterized by simple construction, fast query execution, and strong performance for non-correlated queries. Hybrid range filters integrate two or more of the above filter types, combining their data structures to exploit complementary advantages.

For diverse data distributions and query workloads, selecting an appropriate range filter tailored to the specific application scenario can significantly enhance the system's query efficiency.

1.3 Overview of the Book

Here is the outline of our book. We recommend reading these chapters sequentially.

Chapter 2 introduces some read-only filters step by step. We illustrate Xor filter, Ribbon filter, and Binary Fuse filter, including their design and basic operations. We demonstrate how their designs can conserve more space and reduce query time.

Chapter 3 introduces several space-resilient filters, including Logarithmic Dynamic Cuckoo Filter, Bamboo filter, InfiniFilter, and Variable-length Encoding Framework. We show how their designs can ensure the space resilience of the filters.

Chapter 4 introduces several streaming filters, including Stable Bloom filter, Stable Learned Bloom filter, and Learned Cuckoo filter. We demonstrate how their designs enable the filters to handle unbounded data streams.

Chapter 5 presents various range filters, including prefix-based binary trees or tries, hash-based stacked Bloom filters, monotonic increasing hash functions, hybrid structures, and learning-based linear models.

After reading this book, you will be able to select the most suitable filter when dealing with complex data distribution and query workloads in various system scenarios. Additionally, you will gain some filter design concepts and may be able to design new and efficient filters to handle complex workloads across different systems, access patterns, applications, and devices.

Chapter 2
Read-Only Filters

Abstract Typically, read-only filters are suitable for applications with static and immutable datasets where fast membership queries are essential. The key trait of read-only filters is immutability, meaning elements cannot be added or removed after construction. This immutability enables significant optimization in construction space and query operations. This chapter introduces three representative read-only filters and presents their design trade-offs among space efficiency, construction cost, and query performance.

Keywords Read-only filters · Static datasets

Read-only filters are a class of probabilistic data structures designed to test the membership of a set in static datasets. Once constructed, the filter cannot be modified. Inserts or deletions are not allowed, allowing aggressive space and query time optimizations. It is particularly well-suited for applications requiring high-performance approximate set membership queries over immutable data.

The following sections present several commonly used read-only filters introduced within the past 5 years, including the Xor filter, the Ribbon filter, and the Binary Fuse filter.

2.1 Xor Filter

A Bloom filter enables efficient probabilistic set membership testing while requiring little memory resources. The Bloomier filter represents a conceptual extension of the Bloom filter framework. The Xor filter [1] is a practical implementation of a Bloomier filter variation. Experimental evaluation results show that the Xor filter can achieve superior query speed performance compared to both the Bloom and Cuckoo filters. Also, the Xor filter requires less memory in common use cases.

H. Dai et al., *Advanced Filter Structure Handbook*,
https://doi.org/10.1007/978-981-95-1715-2_2

0	1	2	3	4	5	6	7	8
0010	0001	1010	0000	1101	1011	0101	0000	0100

Fig. 2.1 Example Xor filter

2.1.1 Structure

To put it in a nutshell, the Xor filter consists of an array B whose capacity c marginally exceeds the size of the set $|S|$ ($c \approx 1.23 \times |S|$). Each array element is a k-bit value. Three hash functions h_0, h_1, h_2 will map the set S to three parts of the array ($h_0 : S \rightarrow \{0, ..., c/3 - 1\}, h_1 : S \rightarrow \{c/3, ..., 2c/3 - 1\}, h_2 : S \rightarrow \{2c/3, ..., c - 1\}$).

Figure 2.1 shows an Xor filter with capacity $c = 9$, and the bit length of each array element is $k = 4$. Three hash functions will map set to three ranges $\{0, ..., 2\}, \{3, ..., 5\}, \{6, ..., 8\}$, respectively.

2.1.2 Operation

Xor filter supports two operations: query operation and construction operation.

2.1.2.1 Query

The query operation first calculates the fingerprint of the given key and three hash functions h_0, h_1, h_2 as indexes to the array B and then compares the fingerprint with the exclusive-or result of the corresponding entries in the array B. If the two values are equal, the key is likely in the set S. Algorithm 1 illustrates the query procedure.

2.1.2.2 Construction

The construction operation (Algorithm 2) first randomly selects three hash functions h_0, h_1, h_2, and calls the map function to find the stack σ, which stands for the setup order of the Xor filter. If the stack σ cannot be found, the algorithm will retry the hash function select operation. The hash functions are usually picked by

Algorithm 1 Xor filter query

```
function QUERY(key x)
    return fingerprint(x) = B[h0(x)] xor B[h1(x)] xor B[h2(x)]
end function
```

Algorithm 2 Xor filter construction

```
function CONSTRUCTION(set of keys S)
    repeat
        randomly choose three hash functions h0, h1, h2, without reliance on the fingerprint computation
    until map(S, h0, h1, h2) return success with a stack σ
    B ← an array of length ⌊1.23 · |S|⌋ + 32 storing k-bit values
    for (x, i) in stack σ do
        B[i] ← 0
        B[i] ← fingerprint(x) xor B[h0(x)] xor B[h1(x)] xor B[h2(x)]
    end for
    return the hash functions h0, h1, h2 and B
end function
function MAP(k-bit hash function h0, h1, h2, set of keys S)
    c ← ⌊1.23 · |S|⌋ + 32
    H ← an array of length c storing a vacant set of keys
    for all x in S do
        append x to H[h0(x)]
        append x to H[h1(x)]
        append x to H[h2(x)]
    end for
    Q ← an empty queue
    for i = 0; i < |H|; i + + do
        if |H(i)| equals to 1 then
            add i to Q
        end if
    end for
    while Q is not vacant do
        discard an item i from the queue Q
        if |H(i)| equals to 1 then
            x ← the unique element in the set H(i)
            push the tuple (x, i) onto the stack σ
            for m = 0; m < 3; m++ do
                discard x from the set H[hm(x)]
                if H[hm(x)] equals to 1 then
                    add hm(x) to Q
                end if
            end for
        end if
    end while
    if |σ| equals to |S| then
        return success and the stack σ
    else
        return failure
    end if
end function
```

generating a new pseudorandom seed. After that, an array B of size $\lfloor 1.23 \cdot |S| \rfloor + 32$ is allocated to store the k-bit values. For each (x, i) in the stack, $B[i]$ will be updated according to the key fingerprint and array elements. Finally, the array B and three hash functions h_0, h_1, h_2 are returned as a Xor filter.

A temporary array H is constructed in the map function, consisting of $\lfloor 1.23 \cdot |S| \rfloor + 32$ sets of keys, each of which is initially empty. This function monitors the sets that hold exactly one key. Repeatedly, one of such locations is picked and pushed with the key x to the stack σ. Then the key is removed from its three locations (h_0, h_1, h_2). The process concludes either successfully, yielding a stack that includes all the keys, or indicating failure.

2.1.3 Analysis

Approximately 19% of the entries in the array B are unused; for instance, with 1000 keys, 1230 entries are allocated, leaving 230 empty. A majority of vacant entries in the table B can be relocated to its last third, with slight changes to the construction algorithm. In the map function, three queues instead of one are used. Each hash function uses a unique queue instead of sharing a queue. Entries in the first two queues are handled to completion before processing begins on the third queue. Then the Rank9 data structure can only be used for the last third part of the table, to save space without affecting the speed of the query operation. This variant is referred to as the "Xor+ filter." With the fingerprint size in $\log_2(1/\epsilon)$, the Xor filter needs $1.23\log_2(1/\epsilon)$ bits per item, while the Xor+ filter needs $1.0824\log_2(1/\epsilon) + 0.5125$ bits per item.

2.2 Ribbon Filter

Designed for static sets, the Ribbon filter [2] represents a recent advancement in filter construction. It resembles the Xor filter, with some modifications in the construction algorithm, space configuration, and locality. Compared with other filters, the Ribbon filter can be faster for the same space overhead in many cases.

2.2.1 Structure

The structure of the Ribbon filter is similar to the Xor filter if the Xor filter is represented as a linear system. In the Xor filter, three bits in the coefficient (row) vector $\mathbf{h}(x)$ are assigned the value 1 based on the outputs of three hash functions. The other bits remain in 0. C is the coefficient matrix, derived from the coefficient (row) vectors. B is the fingerprint matrix, composed of the fingerprints $b(x)$. Z is the solution matrix. So the linear system in the Xor filter can be represented as $C \cdot Z = B$. Figure 2.2 shows an example Xor filter represented as a linear system. In this example, three keys produce three coefficient vectors and fingerprints, respectively. The construction operation is responsible for solving this linear system.

$$\begin{matrix}[0,1,0,1,0,0,1,0,0] \\ [0,1,0,0,0,1,1,0,0] \\ [0,0,1,0,0,1,0,1,0]\end{matrix} \cdot Z = \begin{matrix}[1101] \\ [1000] \\ [0111]\end{matrix}$$

Fig. 2.2 A Xor filter, represented as a linear system

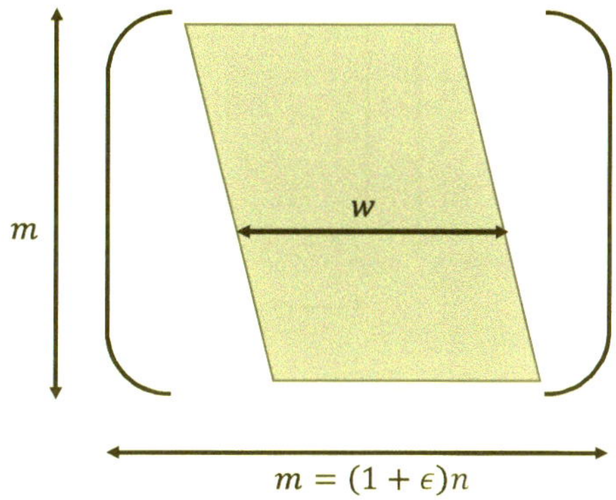

Fig. 2.3 A Ribbon filter coefficient matrix C

The query operation calculates the coefficient vector $\mathbf{h}(x)$ and fingerprint $b(x)$ and compares $\mathbf{h}(x) \cdot Z$ with $b(x)$ (Note that when calculating the matrix multiplication, the add operation is replaced by the xor operation). The solution matrix Z is stored in the row-major layout: the i-th element in the array is the i-th row in Z.

Similar to the Xor filter, the Ribbon filter is the same linear system $C \cdot Z = B$. However, there are still some differences in the coefficient matrix C. Figure 2.3 shows a coefficient matrix C in the Ribbon filter. The length of coefficient vector $\mathbf{h}(x)$ is m. It is given by a random starting point $s(x) \in [m - w - 1]$, together with a randomly generated coefficient vector $c(x) \in \{0, 1\}^w$ (Note that $c(x)$ is forced to start with 1). Therefore, $\mathbf{h}(x)$ can be represented as $0^{s-1}c(x)0^{m-s-w+1}$. The coefficient matrix C is derived from the coefficient vectors $\mathbf{h(x)}_{x \in S}$ with on-the-fly Gaussian elimination. In coefficient matrix C, the i-th row vector is either zero vector $\mathbf{0^w}$, or its first 1 appears at column i. So all of the 1-entries are only presented in a ribbon with width w, from top left to bottom right.

Figure 2.4 represents the linear system of the Ribbon filter. In this linear system, the i-th row either contains nothing ($c_i = 0^w$) or specifies a linear equation $Z_{[i,i+w)} \cdot c_i = b_i$, where c_i starts with a 1, and $Z_{[i,i+w)} \in \{0, 1\}^{w \times r}$ stands for rows $i, \cdots, i + w - 1$ of Z.

In the Xor filter, the memory layout of the solution matrix is row-major. In the Ribbon filter, the memory layout of solution matrix Z can be row-major or column-major. However, both layouts have drawbacks in locality. Interleaved column-major layout (ICML) is proposed to improve locality and reduce memory access counts. It will be discussed further in Sect. 2.2.3.3.

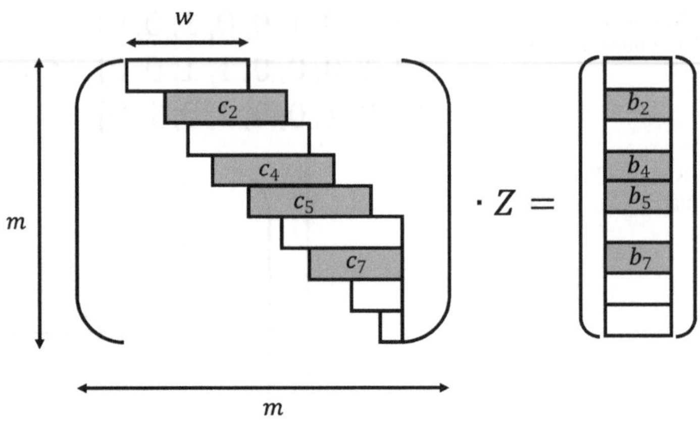

Fig. 2.4 The Ribbon filter linear system *M*

2.2.2 *Operation*

Ribbon filter supports two operations: construction operation and query operation.

2.2.2.1 Construction

The construction operation will start with adding each equation to the linear system. Each equation $(\mathbf{h(x)} \cdot Z = b(x))_{(x \in S)}$ can be added one by one, in arbitrary order with the help of Algorithm 3. The algorithm calculates the row index i, coefficient ribbon c, and fingerprint b and then goes into the loop to add the equation to the linear system. If the i-th row in M is empty, the equation can be added directly. Otherwise, the ribbon $c[i]$ and fingerprint $b[i]$ will be used for Gaussian elimination. Both c and $c[i]$ starts with 1, so c starts with 0 after the elimination. If c and b are 0, this equation can be ignored directly, since it is a redundant equation. If c is 0, but b is not 0, the linear system is not solvable, so the construction is failed. Otherwise, c comprises $j > 0$ zeroes succeeded by a 1. In this case, these leading zeros can be discarded. After updating c and i, another loop will go on. Note that the bit-shift may be reversed because the least significant "first" bit corresponds to the "rightmost" bit in the row vector by convention. Before a key is included in the system, its equation may undergo multiple modifications during the loop. However, it keeps a loop invariant with the following form:

$$c \cdot Z_{[i,i+w)} = b, i \in [m], c \in 1 \circ \{0, 1\}^{w-1}, b \in \{0, 1\}^r \tag{2.1}$$

In the back-substitution phase, due to the coefficient matrix C being a row echelon matrix, when solving the i-th row in solution matrix Z, its dependent rows have already been solved. So the solving process will proceed from bottom to top.

Algorithm 3 Incorporating a key's equation into the linear system M in the Ribbon filter

```
function AddKey(key x)
    i ← s(x)
    c ← c(x)
    b ← b(x)
    loop
        if M.c[i] equals to 0 then
            M.c[i] ← c
            M.b[i] ← b
            return success
        end if
        c ← c ⊕ M.c[i]
        b ← b ⊕ M.b[i]
        if c equals to 0 then
            if b equals to 0 then
                return success // insert a redundant equation
            else
                return failure // insert a inconsistent equation
            end if
        end if
        j ← FirstSet(c) // find the position of first set bit
        i ← i + j
        c ← c >> j // logical shift last toward first
    end loop
end function
```

When solving each column in a row, 0 will be tried first; if the result is different from the expected value in fingerprint matrix B, this bit will be changed to 1.

2.2.2.2 Query

The query operation calculates the ribbon start index $i = s(x)$, coefficient vector $c = c(x)$, and fingerprint value $b = b(x)$. If $c_i \cdot Z_{[i,i+w)}$ equals to b_i, the key x is thought to be in the set.

2.2.3 Analysis

2.2.3.1 Homogeneous Ribbon Filter

When a hash collision occurs, different keys may correspond to the same $vech(x)$ but different $b(x)$, so that the construction of the Ribbon filter encounters a failure. However, when the fingerprint function $b(x)$ only returns 0 for all keys x in the universe, the construction of the Ribbon filter can never fail, because it always has at least the trivial solution $Z = 0^{m \times r}$. This variant of Ribbon filter is called the Homogeneous Ribbon filter.

Though it has at least a solution $Z = 0^{m \times r}$, the filter exhibits a false positive rate of $f_Z = 1$ since every key in the universe yields a calculated fingerprint of 0, which equals the expectation. To solve this issue, all free variables, i.e., the variables corresponding to empty rows of M, are initialized randomly during back-substitution. However, the false positive rate f may exceed 2^{-r}. What's worse, for small key count n, the variance of the false positive rate may reach significant magnitudes. In other words, the filter may have significantly more false positives than expected.

The space efficiency for Homogeneous Ribbon filter satisfies Theorem 2.1 (Note that the space overhead is $\frac{SPACE}{OPT} - 1$ where $SPACE$ denotes the filter's actual space consumption in bits per key and $OPT = -\log_2(f)$ represents the theoretical lower bound required for any filter achieving identical false positive rate):

Theorem 2.1 *There exists $C \in R^+$ such that for any $\epsilon < 1/2$, $\frac{m}{n} = 1 + \epsilon$, any desired false positive rate $\varphi > 0$ and r the closest integer to $-\log_2(\phi)$ the following holds. For any $w \in N$ with $\epsilon w > Cmax(\log w, r)$ and $n \in N$, the Homogeneous Ribbon filter with n keys and parameters ϵ, w, r has $f \in [\varphi/2, 2\varphi]$ and space overhead at most 2ϵ.*

According to Theorem 2.1, the space overhead can be represented as $rm/n \log f^{-1} - 1 = r(1 + \epsilon)/\log f^{-1} - 1$. To minimize the space overhead for chosen values of r and w, ϵ must be neither too large nor too small (small ϵ causes false positive rate to explode). Based on the simulations of random data, a pattern to minimize for any large n is found as follows:

$$\epsilon = \frac{4 + r/4}{w} \tag{2.2}$$

2.2.3.2 Configurability and Elasticity

The Bloom filter can efficiently utilize any amount of space to minimize the false positive rate. However, some alternatives, such as Cuckoo, Quotient, and Xor, often use cells of some whole number of bits r. It limits space-efficient choices to attain an equivalent false positive rate with less space. For example, if $r = 4.5$ can satisfy the false positive requirement for a specific application, r can only choose 5 because it cannot be a fractional number in these Bloom filter alternatives conventionally, adding roughly 10% space overhead. Some variants of these alternatives propose fractional-bit cell sizes, but they are usually neither general nor efficient.

A way of implementing a general and effective fractional cell size r is splitting space into two structures: one uses $\lceil r \rceil$ cell size, while the other uses $\lfloor r \rfloor$ cell size, and then a weighted average bit per cell r can be achieved. However, splitting into two structures may double the space usage penalties associated with small structures and decrease the probability of joint construction.

In the Ribbon filter, a variant of this approach is taken: in a single structure, there are $\lfloor r \rfloor$ bits for each slot in some prefix of rows, $\lceil r \rceil$ bits in the remaining rows. This approach does not need to change the banding Algorithm 3, but the back-substitution and query algorithm needs to be changed slightly. With this approach, the w/m portion of queries will cross the boundary between $\lfloor r \rfloor$ and $\lceil r \rceil$ columns. In this scenario, only $\lfloor r \rfloor$ bits will be used.

This single-structure approach brings another advantage: elasticity. Similar to the Xor filter, an entire column in solution vector Z can be dropped, so that the filter can be trimmed down with a higher false positive rate. A finished Ribbon filter (except the Homogeneous Ribbon filter) can be split into several smaller structures with independent false positive rates. By duplicating as little as $(w - 1)r$ bits at the partition boundary, the Ribbon filter can be partitioned, and each query only accesses one partition.

2.2.3.3 Memory Layout of Solution Matrix

In the Xor filter, a row-major layout is used to store the solution matrix. In other words, the $i + 1$-th row of Z is stored after the whole of the i-th row. For each query, the Xor filter only accesses three rows in the solution matrix, so the memory access count is not quite high. However, in the Ribbon filter, the number of solution columns is usually $5 \leq r \leq 15$, while the ribbon width is usually $w \in 16, 32, 64, 128$. So a row-major-based memory layout incurs much more access counts.

The opposite memory layout is the column-major layout, in which the entire column i precedes column $i + 1$ in memory. In this memory layout, the query algorithm can get contiguous w bits, bitwise-AND with coefficient vector $c(x)$, and get the bit parity as the single result bit of a key. However, accessing w bits in each column is not adjacent. Though the several memory addresses are easily computed and can be fetched in parallel, it is still a relatively expensive operation.

The solution for the Ribbon filter is interleaved column-major layout (ICML), shown in Fig. 2.5. In this memory layout, each column is divided into w bits ICML words and then grouped into blocks of r words. Each block is the column-major layout of some contiguous rows of Z. Figure 2.5 generalizes this layout for fractional column size r, achieving better reconfigurability. In this layout, $\lfloor r \rfloor$ size columns are placed before $\lceil r \rceil$ size columns. Upon the starting memory location and an applicable number of columns are calculated, the remaining query code does not have to be aware of mixed numbers of columns. So the ICML layout can support clean configurability to achieve better space efficiency.

ICML layout has a better locality than row-major and column-major layout. For ICML word size equal to w, at most two continuous words ($2rw$ bits) are combined for reconstructing each result bit, while the ideal minimum is one word (rw bits). Also, it can support short-circuiting in query operations: return the key does not exist when the result bit is not expected, similar to the column-major memory layout.

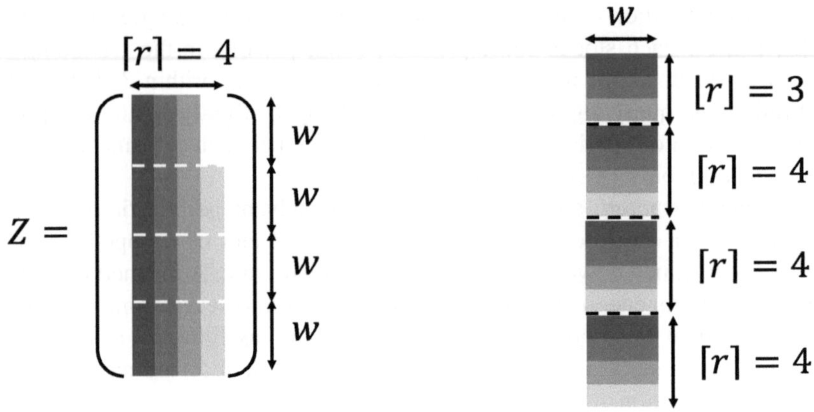

Fig. 2.5 ICML format in Ribbon filter

In a word, it has better locality than the column-major layout, while its decoding efficiency is close to the column-major layout.

2.3 Binary Fuse Filter

As an extension of the Xor filter, the structure proposed in [3] defines the Binary Fuse filter. Though it shares a similar conceptual foundation and depend on almost identical straightforward code, the Binary Fuse filter offers higher time efficiency than the Xor filter, with a smaller overhead on memory usage. Furthermore, if the 3-wise construction in the Binary Fuse filter is replaced by the 4-wise construction, the space overhead can be further reduced. When minimizing the space overhead is considered to be the most important factor, it is more feasible than the Xor filter.

2.3.1 Structure

The Binary Fuse filter shares a comparable memory layout with the Xor filter. Specifically, the Binary Fuse filter is an array B with capacity c. Each array element is a k-bit value. Different from the Xor filter, the array is divided into many (e.g., hundreds) small same-size nonoverlapping segments. Three hash functions h_0, h_1, h_2 will map the set S to three indexes, each in a consecutive distinct segment in the Binary Fuse filter. In 4-wise construction, the count of hash functions and segments will be switched from three to four.

Figure 2.6 shows a Binary Fuse filter with capacity $c = 9$, and the bit length of each array element is $k = 4$. The filter is divided into three segments

0	1	2	3	4	5	6	7	8
1000	0000	0010	1010	1001	1011	0010	0001	1100

Fig. 2.6 Example Binary Fuse filter

Algorithm 4 Binary Fuse filter query

```
function QUERY(key x)
    return fingerprint(x) = B[h0(x)] xor B[h1(x)] xor B[h2(x)]
end function
```

{0, ..., 2}, {3, ..., 5}, {6, ..., 8}. Three hash functions will map keys to three consecutive distinct segments, respectively.

2.3.2 *Operation*

The Binary Fuse filter supports two operations: query operation and construction operation.

2.3.2.1 Query

Similar to the Xor filter, the query operation first calculates the fingerprint of the given key and three hash functions h_0, h_1, h_2 as indexes to the array B and then compares the fingerprint with the exclusive-or result of the corresponding entries in the array B. The algorithm procedure is shown in Algorithm 4.

2.3.2.2 Construction

The construction operation (Algorithm 5) first initializes a fingerprint function F and an array H to store the filter. Then three hash functions h_0, h_1, h_2 are randomly chosen, to associate a given key with three adjacent segments within the array. After that, the key set is partially sorted according to the index of the segments containing the array index $h_0(x)$. This can be accomplished in linear complexity through a single traversal, due to the limited number of segments.

The sorted set can be scanned through to update an array of sets. This set can be realized via a zero-initialized integer counter and a fixed-size mask. When a key is added, the counter is incremented and the mask is updated through an exclusive with the key. Similarly, removing a key decrements the counter and updates the mask via an XOR with the key. If the set contains a single element, the mask equals that element. Since the keys are organized by segment, the sets array is traversed sequentially, which lowers cache miss rates relative to random access. This array

Algorithm 5 Binary Fuse filter construction

function CONSTRUCTION(set of keys S)
  $n \leftarrow |S|$
  $F \leftarrow$ a fingerprint function to map keys to k-bit integers which determines the false-positive probability $(\epsilon = 1/2^k)$
  $H \leftarrow$ a zero-initialized array of length $c \approx 1.125n$ including k-bit values, divided into segments of size $2^{\lfloor \log_{3.33} n + 2.25 \rfloor}$
  repeat
    randomly choose three hash functions h_0, h_1, h_2, mapping keys to array indexes so that these indexes occupy three consecutive distinct segments.
    sort the key set S according to the index of segment corresponding to array index $h_0(x)$: keys mapping to the first segment should be placed at first, followed sequentially by those assigned to subsequent segments
    $B \leftarrow$ an array of vacant sets with the same length with H
    scan through the sorted set S, add each key x to sets $B[h_0(x)]$, $B[h_1(x)]$, $B[h_2(x)]$
    $Q \leftarrow$ an empty stack containing the indexes
    traverse array B sequentially, push each singleton index into Q
    $P \leftarrow$ an empty stack containing the keys and indexes
    while Q is not vacant **do**
      $i \leftarrow$ an index popped from Q
      if $B[i]$ is sole **then**
        push x as well as the index i pair (x, i) into stack P, where the key x is contained in $B[i]$
        for m = 0; m < 3; m++ **do**
          remove x from the set $B[h_m(x)]$
          if $B[h_m(x)]$ is sole **then**
            add $h_m(x)$ to Q
          end if
        end for
      end if
    end while
  until the length of P equals n
  for (x, i) in stack P **do**
    $H[i] \leftarrow$ fingerprint(x) xor $H[h_0(x)]$ xor $H[h_1(x)]$ xor $H[h_2(x)]$
  end for
  return the hash functions h_0, h_1, h_2 and H
end function

will be scanned later to find the index of the singleton and push it to the stack Q. Since the array is scanned forward, keys appearing later in the stack are more likely to be associated with higher indexes.

After that, the stack Q is unwound, virtually popping the indexes, and conditionally adding the new singleton. These popped indexes will be added to another P. This procedure typically accesses the sets array B in reverse order. Finally, the Binary Fuse filter is constructed according to the stack P, with the exclusive or result of values from three indexes and the key fingerprint. This process tends to traverse the filter array H forward, from the beginning to the end.

2.3.3 *Analysis*

2.3.3.1 4-Wise Binary Fuse Filter

If three hash functions are replaced with four hash functions, the filter array size can be further reduced. The resulting data structure is called the 4-wise Binary Fuse Filter. The space overhead of the Binary Fuse filter and 4-wise Binary Fuse filter is discussed in Sect. 2.3.3.2. The construction and member query algorithm in a 4-wise Binary Fuse filter is similar to that of a Binary Fuse filter, except each key is mapped to four indexes instead of three.

2.3.3.2 Space Overhead and Segment Size

A 3-wise Binary Fuse filter array's size is $\left\lfloor 0.875+0.25\max\left(1, \frac{\log 10^6}{\log n}\right)\right\rfloor$, while that of a 4-wise Binary Fuse filter is $\left\lfloor 0.77+0.305\max\left(1, \frac{\log 6\cdot 10^5}{\log n}\right)\right\rfloor$. According to the formulas, the array size converges to $\lfloor 1.125n \rfloor$ for 3-wise and $\lfloor 1.075n \rfloor$ for 4-wise as the set becomes large. The segment sizes are $2^{\lfloor \log_{3.33} n+2.25 \rfloor} \approx 4.8 \cdot n^{0.58}$ (3-wise) and $2^{\lfloor \log_{2.91} n-0.5 \rfloor} \approx 0.7 \cdot n^{0.65}$ (4-wise). In practice, the array size is rounded up to be a multiple of the segment length. Furthermore, in the 3-wise scenario, there are a minimum of three segments, whereas in the 4-wise scenario, there are at least four segments. In simulations, a filter with parameters configured according to these formulas exhibits a failure probability below 1%, often significantly lower than this threshold.

2.4 Summary and Comparison

2.4.1 *Summary of Read-Only Filters*

The Xor filter, Ribbon filter, and Binary Fuse filter represent recent advances in the design of read-only filter. These filters leverage the immutability of the input set to achieve significant gains in space efficiency and query throughput compared to traditional dynamic structures like the Bloom filter. While the Xor filter introduces a simple and effective approach with strong performance characteristics for low false positive rates, the Ribbon filter emphasizes memory access locality, making it well-suited for storage systems with hierarchical memory. The Binary Fuse filter builds on the principles of the Xor filter and pushes the boundaries of space efficiency even further. Together, these filters offer a diverse set of trade-offs and implementation strategies tailored for static membership testing in modern systems. The next section provides a comparative analysis of these filters, highlighting their strengths and limitations.

Table 2.1 Comparison of read-only filters

Filter	Dynamic insertion	Memory access	False positive rate
Bloom filter	✓	k	$\left(1 - e^{-\frac{kn}{m}}\right)^k$
Xor filter	✗	3	$\left(2^{l_f}\right)^{-1}$
Ribbon filter	✗	1	$\left(2^{l_f}\right)^{-1}$
Binary Fuse filter	✗	3 or 4	$\left(2^{l_f}\right)^{-1}$

2.4.2 Comparison of Read-Only Filters

Table 2.1 summarizes three key features of Bloom filter and the three read-only filters [4]. (1) Xor filter generally uses less memory than Bloom filter under a low false positive rate (i.e., $\leq 3\%$). Besides, Xor filter offers faster query throughput than Bloom filter. Notably, it is designed for the static set, adding or deleting elements after construction typically requires rebuilding the entire filter. (2) Ribbon filter is designed to maximize data locality, which can lead to better cache performance during queries. They are particularly well-suited for immutable data resources in systems like LSM-trees. (3) Binary fuse filter is an evolution of Xor filter, designed to be even more space efficient, often achieving memory usage closer to the theoretical lower bound compared to Xor filters.

2.4.3 Conclusion

For Xor, Ribbon, and Binary Fuse filters, their goal is to achieve superior space efficiency and often faster query performance compared to Bloom filters for a given false positive rate. While Xor filters improve space and lookup speed, Ribbon filters offer a more appropriate balance of space and time with greater configurability. The Binary Fuse filter achieves even greater space efficiency and faster construction times by optimizing the underlying hashing and peeling process. In essence, these newer filters offer more refined and performant solutions for membership testing in scenarios where the dataset is known at construction time, making them increasingly attractive choices for applications demanding the utmost in memory conservation and speed.

References

1. Graf, T.M., Lemire, D.: Xor filters. ACM J. Exp. Algorithmics **25**, 1–16 (2020)
2. Dillinger, P.C., Walzer, S.: Ribbon filter: practically smaller than Bloom and Xor. CoRR abs/2103.02515 (2021)

3. Graf, T.M., Lemire, D.: Binary fuse filters: fast and smaller than Xor filters. ACM J. Exp. Algorithmics **27**, 1.5:1–1.5:15 (2022)
4. Martínez, R., Reviriego, P., Larrabeiti, D.: Supporting dynamic insertions in Xor and binary fuse filters with the integrated xor/BIF-Bloom filter. IEEE Trans. Netw. Serv. Manag. **21**(3), 3068–3079 (2024)

Chapter 3
Space-Resilient Filters

Abstract Conventional filter data structures typically have a fixed memory footprint set during construction, making them unsuitable for dynamic datasets with frequently changing element counts. To address this, space-resilient filters have been developed, designed to adapt to fluctuating dataset sizes while ensuring high query efficiency and minimal space overhead. This chapter introduces four representative structures and provides their core design insight.

Keywords Space-resilient filters · Dynamic set representation · Expandability · Data growth

Filter data structures typically require the dataset size to be predetermined at construction time. However, when facing dynamic datasets in real-world scenarios [1, 2], they often encounter the contradiction between "static space allocation" and "dynamic demands." For instance, the Bloom filter necessitates predefining its capacity and allocating fixed space. Once the inserted element count exceeds the predefined size, its false positive rate significantly increases. Conversely, pre-specifying a larger capacity during construction can mitigate the degradation of false positive rates but inevitably leads to considerable space waste.

Space-resilient filters are designed to address this challenge. They can adapt to variations in the number of elements by employing hierarchical structures, chained architectures, and adaptive encoding schemes, maintaining high query efficiency and low space overhead. This effectively resolves the limitations of traditional filter data structures in dynamic dataset scenarios.

This section focuses on four representative structures that reconstruct the design philosophy of space-resilient filters from different dimensions:

- **Logarithmic Dynamic Cuckoo Filter** (LDCF) [3] reorganizes multiple Cuckoo filters into a treelike structure, reducing the number of filters accessed for each operation from linear complexity in chained structures to logarithmic complexity.
- **Bamboo filter** [4] employs a segmented storage architecture combining hash tables and segments, reorganizing multiple Cuckoo filters into a linear array and reducing the number of filters accessed during operations to a constant level.

H. Dai et al., *Advanced Filter Structure Handbook*,
https://doi.org/10.1007/978-981-95-1715-2_3

- **InfiniFilter** [5] integrates expansion mechanisms with chained structures, achieving infinite scalability while maintaining stable false positive rates.
- **Variable-Length Encoding Framework** [6] designs an adaptive encoding scheme for various filters, mitigating space waste when filters are configured with large capacities.

3.1 Logarithmic Dynamic Cuckoo Filter

Filters typically require a predefined capacity to function effectively. To facilitate evolving data volumes, the Dynamic Cuckoo Filter (DCF) [7] is introduced. However, its linear chaining architecture inherently causes computational and memory requirements to increase proportionally with dataset size, making it unsuitable for handling large-scale dynamic workloads. The Logarithmic Dynamic Cuckoo Filter (LDCF) [3] addresses this limitation through a hierarchical tree framework, achieving logarithmic time complexity for operations while significantly improving memory efficiency compared to its predecessor.

3.1.1 Structure: Filters in a Tree

LDCF arranges multiple CFs in a hierarchical tree structure. Figure 3.1a shows an example of the basic LDCF. On the level l, there are 2^l CFs. The notation CF_p^q denotes the q-th CF on the p-th level. Each CF_p^q contains t buckets, with b entries

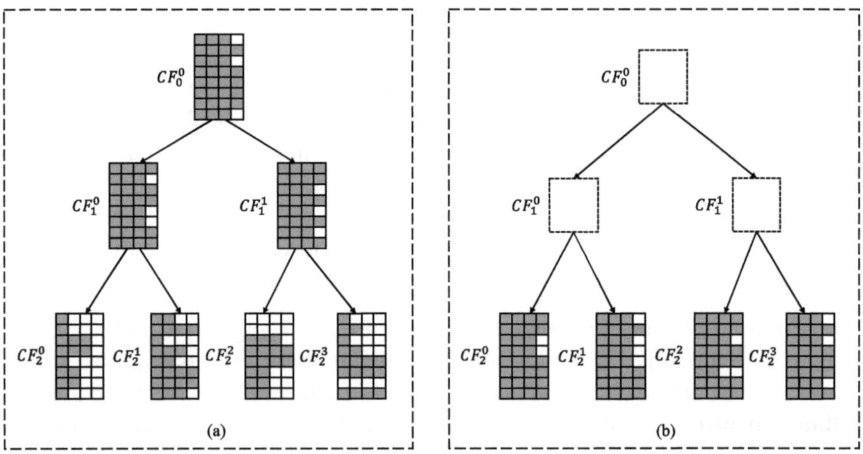

Fig. 3.1 LDCF structure. (**a**) The structure of basic LDCF. (**b**) The structure of compacted LDCF

in each bucket. Initially, the LDCF has only one CF: CF_0^0. To insert an element x, its fingerprint ξ_x is placed into an unoccupied slot within the designated bucket. When the insertion operation fails, two first-level CFs, i.e. CF_1^0 and CF_1^1, are added as the children node of CF_0^0, to extend the capacity of the LDCF. Afterward, the insertion operations are performed on the first-level CFs. During the insertion process, the first bit of ξ_x is checked. If the first bit is "0," the fingerprint is inserted into CF_1^0; otherwise, it is inserted into CF_1^1. Therefore, the first bit of ξ_x does not need to be stored in the first-level CFs, and one bit in each entry can be saved, compared with the CF_0^0. Similarly, when the first-level CFs are full, four second-level CFs, i.e. CF_2^0, CF_2^1, CF_2^2, and CF_2^3, are added. Then fingerprints with the prefixes "00," "01," "10," and "11" are added to CF_2^0, CF_2^1, CF_2^2 and CF_2^3, respectively, and two bits can be saved for entries in the second-level CFs. Generally, in the i-th level, there are 2^i CFs, and i bits can be eliminated in these CFs.

During LDCF expansion, newly created CFs at higher levels remain underutilized because few fingerprints are stored in them. Therefore, it may lead to suboptimal space utilization compared to DCF. To further reduce the space overhead, a compacted LDCF is proposed. Figure 3.1b presents an example of the compacted LDCF. It keeps the same multi-level tree structure as the basic LDCF. However, only leaf nodes in the tree are CFs, while other nodes keep pointers to their two children. Initially, there is only one root node CF_0^0 in the tree, which is also a leaf node. When a leaf node CF_p^q cannot accommodate the inserted fingerprints, it creates two child CFs, i.e. CF_{p+1}^{2q} and CF_{p+1}^{2q+1}, migrates the fingerprints in it to these CFs, and deletes itself. Thus, higher space utilization can be achieved.

3.1.2 Support Operation

The LDCF supports five operations: insertion operation, append operation, query operation, deletion operation, and compression operation.

3.1.2.1 Insertion

The insertion operation is described in Algorithm 6. It first initializes the visiting level in the multi-level tree $curLevel$, current CF node $curLoc$, key fingerprint ξ_e, and the indexes of the candidate bucket μ_e and ν_e. After that, the multi-level tree is visited to find the CF to insert the fingerprint and its corresponding level. Then the key relocation is started. If the destination bucket contains at least one available entry, the fingerprint ξ_e is stored in it. Otherwise, a randomly selected fingerprint ξ_x is evicted and will be tried to insert into another candidate bucket. Finally, if $curCF$ is full, the two child CFs will be appended after it.

Figure 3.2 demonstrates an example of the insertion operations. Since no CF exists on levels 0 and 1, CF_2^2 is located based on the binary prefix 10 of the

Algorithm 6 Insert a key to the LDCF

```
function INSERT(key e)
    curLevel ← 0
    curLoc ← root
    ξ_e ← fingerprint(e)
    μ_e ← hash(e)
    ν_e ← μ_e⊕ hash(ξ_e)
    while curLoc.CF is NULL do
        curLevel ← curLevel + 1
        prefix ← getPrefix(ξ_e, curLevel)
        curLoc ← getChild(curLoc, curLevel, prefix)
    end while
    curCF ← curLoc.CF
    bucket ← randomly choose μ_e or ν_e
    for iter = 0; iter < THRESHOLD; iter + + do
        ξ_e ← cutPrefix(ξ_e, curLevel)
        if an unoccupied entry is found in bucket then
            store ξ_e in the bucket
            break
        end if
        ξ_x ← randomly selected entry from bucket in curCF
        victim ← ξ_x
        replace ξ_x with ξ_e
        victim ← addPrefix(victim, pre)
        bucket ← bucket⊕ hash(victim)
    end for
    if curCF is full then
        curLoc ← Append(curCF, curLevel)
    end if
end function
```

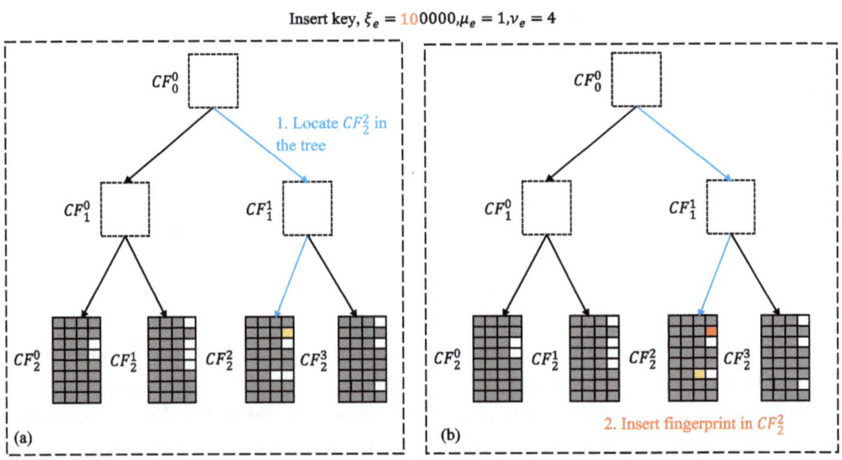

Fig. 3.2 An insertion example on LDCF. (**a**) Before insert. (**b**) After insert

fingerprint ξ_e. Both destination buckets in CF_2^2 are fully occupied. To resolve this conflict, the algorithm relocates the entry marked in yellow to an alternative bucket within the same CF, thereby creating space for the newly inserted fingerprint marked in orange.

3.1.2.2 Append

When a leaf-level CF reaches its capacity, the LDCF initiates a hierarchical expansion by allocating two child CFs at the next level. The process is described in Algorithm 7. After these new CFs are initialized, fingerprints in the parent CF should be migrated to these new CFs, according to the prefix of the fingerprints. For instance, consider fingerprints $\xi_{e0} = 01000, \xi_{e_1} = 10110, \xi_{e_2} = 10011, \xi_{e_3} = 01111$ produced by four elements $e_i(i = 0, 1, 2, 3)$ in CF_1^0, ξ_{e0}, and ξ_{e_3} need to be migrated to the 0-child CF, and ξ_{e_1} and ξ_{e_2} need to be migrated to CF_2^1. Finally, the parent CF is deleted to improve the space efficiency of the LDCF.

To speed up the migration process, an efficient bit-wise operation is adopted to quickly remove fingerprints whose prefix does not match the child CF. During the fingerprint migration process in LDCF, the contents of the parent Cuckoo filter (CF) are distributed to two child CFs. Once the child CFs are populated, each fingerprint in the 0-child CF is updated according to the equation $\xi = \xi\&(1 << (l' - 1) - (\sim \xi >> (l' - 1))\&1)$, where l' is the current length of fingerprint in the parent CF. Figure 3.3 illustrates the migration process with an example. In the example, l' equals 5. For the 0-child CF, if ξ starts with 0, ξ is updated according to $\xi = \xi\&01111$, and the last 4 bits are kept in the entry. However, if ξ starts with 1, ξ is updated according to $\xi = \xi\&10000$, and the last 4 bits are cleared in the entry. Therefore, only the fingerprints with the expected prefix are kept in the bucket. Similarly, for the 1-child CF, each fingerprint is updated according to the equation $\xi = \xi\&(1 << (l' - 1) - (\xi >> (l' - 1))\&1)$ to evict the fingerprints with the prefix 0.

Algorithm 7 Append children CFs to the LDCF

---

function APPEND(LDCF node Loc, the level of the filter $level$)
  $f \leftarrow$ the fingerprint length in the root CF
  $newlevel \leftarrow level + 1$
  initialize empty LDCF node $Loc.0child$ and $Loc.1child$
  $Loc.0child.CF \leftarrow$ a new Cuckoo filter with the same bucket and entry count, storing $(f - newlevel)$ bits fingerprint
  $Loc.1child.CF \leftarrow$ a new Cuckoo filter with the same bucket and entry count, storing $(f - newlevel)$ bits fingerprint
  for each fingerprint ξ in $Loc.CF$ **do**
    migrate to $Loc.0child.CF$ or $Loc.1child.CF$
  end for
  delete $Loc.CF$
  $Loc.CF \leftarrow$ NULL
end function

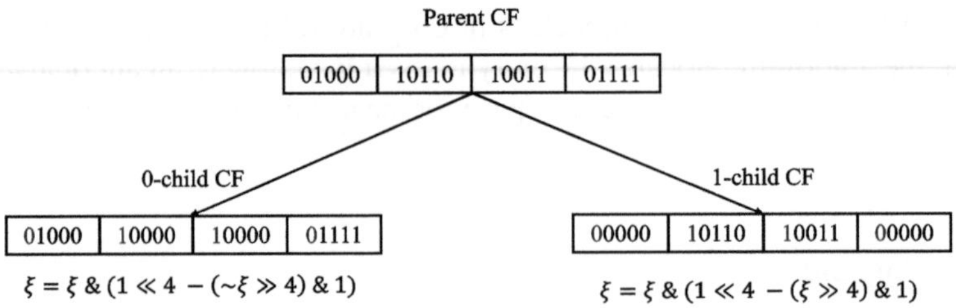

Fig. 3.3 LDCF parallel migration

Algorithm 8 Query a key in the LDCF

```
function QUERY(key e)
    ξ_e ← fingerprint(e)
    μ_e ← hash(e)
    ν_e ← μ_e⊕ hash(ξ_e)
    for i = 0; i < curLDCF.level; i ++ do
        prefix ← getPrefix(ξ_e, i)
        curCF ← curLDCF.getCF(i, prefix)
        if curCF is NULL then
            continue
        end if
        ξ ← cutPrefix(ξ_e, i)
        if bucket μ_e or ν_e in curCF contains ξ then
            return true
        end if
    end for
    return false
end function
```

3.1.2.3 Query

Algorithm 8 describes the query operation in the LDCF. First, the key fingerprint ξ_e and the indexes of the candidate bucket μ_e and ν_e are calculated. After that, it employs a hierarchical traversal strategy, similar to that of the insertion operation. At every level, a single CF is examined based on the prefix of the queried element's fingerprint. In the compacted LDCF, if the node does not have the corresponding CF, the operation keeps searching for the element in the next level. Otherwise, the fingerprint without the i bit prefix is checked on the CF, where i is the level of the CF. It returns true when a matched fingerprint is found.

3.1.2.4 Deletion

The deletion operation is described in Algorithm 9. To delete the key e from the LDCF, a query operation is performed first. If a fingerprint is found in a CF, it will be removed by setting all the remaining bits to "0."

Algorithm 9 Delete a key from the LDCF

```
function DELETE(key e)
    ξ_e ← fingerprint(e)
    μ_e ← hash(e)
    ν_e ← μ_e⊕ hash(ξ_e)
    for i = 0; i < curLDCF.level; i + + do
        prefix ← getPrefix(ξ_e, i)
        curCF ← curLDCF.getCF(i, prefix)
        if curCF is NULL then
            continue
        end if
        ξ ← cutPrefix(ξ_e, i)
        if bucket μ_e or ν_e in curCF contains ξ then
            remove ξ
            return true
        end if
    end for
    return false
end function
```

3.1.2.5 Compression

If the application performs deletion operations more frequently than insertion operations, a compression operation can be performed to save space. The compaction operation becomes feasible when, for every bucket, the combined fingerprint count in both child CFs does not exceed the bucket capacity of the parent CF. The operation transfers all fingerprints from the child CFs to the parent CF and adds a prefix bit to each fingerprint according to its original child CF (0 for the left child, 1 for the right child).

3.1.3 Theoretical Analysis

3.1.3.1 False Positive Rate

The DCF requires checking all CFs in the chain during queries, whereas the compacted LDCF only needs to examine a single leaf-node CF. In a LDCF with l_c levels and initial fingerprint length f, leaf-node fingerprints have a reduced length of $f - l_c$. Consequently, each entry has a false match probability of $\frac{1}{2^{f-l_c}}$ for nonexistent elements. Thus, the false positive rate is attained as follows:

$$\epsilon_{LDCF_{compact}} = 1 - \left(1 - \frac{1}{2^{f-l_c}}\right)^{2b} \approx \frac{2b}{2^{f-l_c}} \tag{3.1}$$

3.1.3.2 Computation Cost of Membership Checking

During query operations, the LDCF structure enables efficient lookups by checking only one CF per level. Consider a 3-level basic LDCF with element e having a 6-bit fingerprint $\xi_e = 011110$, the root CF, the "0"-branch CF on level 1, the "01"-branch CF on level 2, and the "011"-branch CF on level 3 are visited. For a basic LDCF with l levels, queries examine at most $l + 1$ CFs in the worst case. In a compacted LDCF, only one CF is checked for each query operation.

3.1.3.3 Space Efficiency and Utilization

The LDCF structure achieves space savings by reducing fingerprint length by i bits at each level i. Therefore, for a compacted LDCF with l levels, the total space cost is $2^l * c * (f - l)$ bits, where f is the fingerprint length of the CF_0^0, and c is the number of entries in a CF. In comparison, a DCF with a total number of 2^l CFs has a total space cost of $2^l * c * f$ bits. This leads to a space cost ratio between LDCF and DCF less than $\frac{f-l}{f}$, proving that LDCF provides superior space efficiency while maintaining equivalent capacity.

Space utilization quantifies the occupancy rate of stored fingerprints within the allocated storage capacity. The insertion process continues until reaching a maximum load factor threshold (e.g., 95%). When this threshold is exceeded in a CF, an append operation triggers redistribution of elements from the parent CF to its child CFs. This expansion increases the capacity of LDCF by up to twice and reduces space utilization but maintains $\geq$47.5%.

While deletions lower space utilization, LDCF handles them more efficiently than DCF by retaining deleted slots for reuse. This design maintains insertion flexibility without permanent capacity loss. When higher utilization is required, the structure supports on-demand compression to optimize space usage.

3.2 Bamboo Filter

Resizing operations (e.g., expansion or compaction) in dynamic filter structures introduce performance bottlenecks. First, when a resizing operation is initiated, other operations cannot proceed until the resizing completes. For example, in LDCF, the resizing operation requires transferring all the fingerprints from the parent CF to the two child CFs. During this phase, other operations on the affected CFs have to wait for the resizing process. In addition, multiple resizing operations lead to the performance degradation of the filter structure. For instance, frequent resizing operations escalate the hierarchical depth of the LDCF tree. As the depth increases, each operation requires traversing more levels, leading to throughput degradation.

The Bamboo filter [4] is proposed to alleviate the two problems in dynamic filters. It employs a fine-grained resizing operation to minimize the duration of the operation blocking. Furthermore, it achieves constant-time complexity for insertion, search, and deletion operations regardless of the number of prior resizing events.

3.2.1 Structure: Filters in a Linear Hash Table

The Bamboo filter is a four-layer structure consisting of a hash table, segments, buckets, and entries. A hash table organizes multiple segments. Each segment is the basic unit of resizing, and a segment is added in each expansion operation. A segment resembles a Cuckoo filter and contains a series of buckets. A bucket comprises several entries. Each entry stores a fingerprint in it. Figure 3.4 shows an example of the Bamboo filter. In this example, a segment contains four buckets, and a bucket comprises four entries.

A segment is overflow if no more fingerprints can be stored in it. In the Bamboo filter, segments with a smaller index in the hash table are expanded earlier. During an expansion operation, fingerprints in the segment are rehashed and redistributed into different segments, even if the segment is not overflowing. If the overflow segment cannot be resized in time, another segment will be inserted after the overflow segment to store the fingerprints, and an overflow segment list is formed. This resize strategy is called "partial-key linear hashing," and it helps achieve constant-time operations. Figure 3.4 illustrates an overflow segment list comprising four segments, where each expansion appends a new segment to the end of the hash table. To streamline the discussion, a round of expansion is proposed. For a Bamboo filter with $2^i N_0$ segments (where N_0 is the base number of segments and i is a nonnegative integer), when $2^i N_0$ expansion operations are executed on each segment, there will be $2^{i+1} N_0$ segments afterward. This sequence of operations is defined as the $i + 1$-th round of expansion.

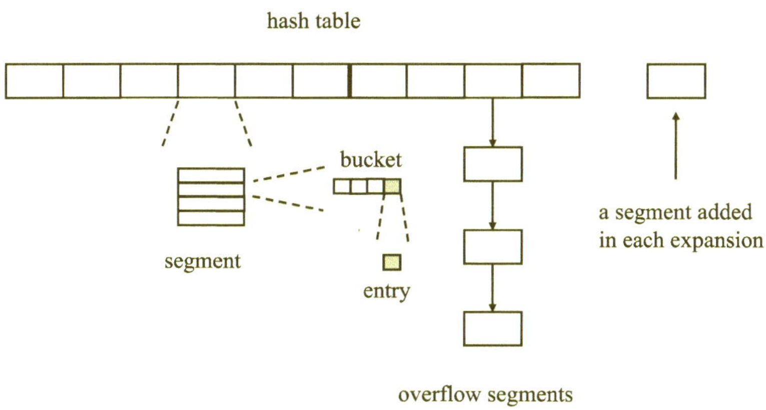

Fig. 3.4 Bamboo filter structure

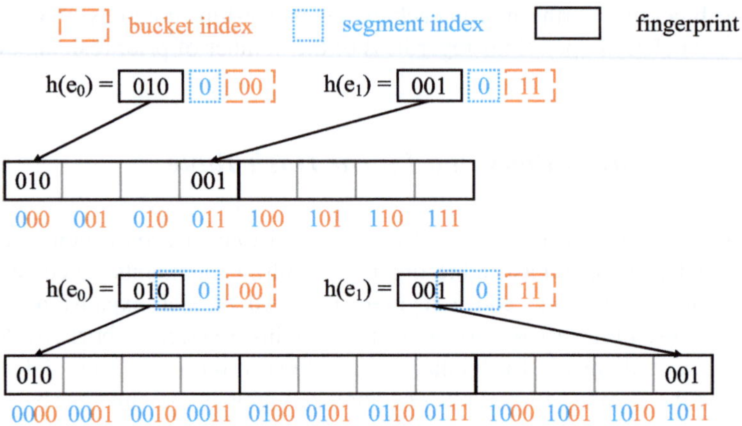

Fig. 3.5 Bamboo filter index sharing example

For Cuckoo filters, only the fingerprints (truncated hash values) of inserted keys are stored, which inherently prevents reconstruction of the original key. This limitation becomes apparent during resizing, as relocating a fingerprint to a new bucket requires knowledge of the original key, which is unavailable.

The Bamboo filter tackles this challenge by splitting the hash value of the key into the bucket index, the segment index, and the fingerprint while enabling bit-sharing between the fingerprint and segment index. This approach, termed "index-sharing," allows the Bamboo filter to dynamically resize without the need for storing the original key.

Figure 3.5 illustrates an expansion operation. Initially, the filter comprises two segments, each with four buckets. Fingerprints for elements e_0 and e_1 reside in separate buckets within segment 0. During expansion, a new segment is added. To rehash fingerprints, the segment index length is incremented by 1 bit, borrowing a bit from the fingerprint. Consequently, e_1's fingerprint is rehashed into the new segment based on the updated segment index.

3.2.2 *Operation*

The Bamboo filter supports five operations: insertion operation, expansion operation, query operation, deletion operation, and compression operation.

3.2.2.1 Insertion

The insertion operation is described in Algorithm 10. It first calculates the fingerprint f, segment index I_s, bucket index I_b, and $I_{b'}$ of the key e. Given the I_b length

Algorithm 10 Insert a key to the Bamboo filter

```
function INSERT(key e)
    calculate f, I_b, I'_b, I_s according to key e
    if segment[I_s].bucket[I_b] or segment[I_s].bucket[I'_b] is not full then
        find an unoccupied slot in one of these buckets to store f
        goto CheckExpand
    end if
    i_b ← randomly selected bucket from I_b or I'_b
    while the iteration count does not exceed the threshold M_e do
        e ← randomly selected entry from i_b
        swap f and the fingerprint from e
        i'_b ← another candidate bucket of f
        if segment[I_s].bucket[i'_b] is not full then
            find an unoccupied slot in segment[I_s].bucket[i'_b] to store f
            goto CheckExpand
        end if
        i_b ← i'_b
    end while
    insert f into the overflow chain of segment[I_s]
CheckExpand:
    invoke Expand() if the expansion is triggered
    return success
end function
```

l_b, the I_f length l_f, and the I_s original length (without segment expansion) l_{s0}, f, I_b and $I_{b'}$ can be calculated with the following equations:

$$f(e) = (hash(e) >> (l_b + l_{s0})) \mod 2^{l_f}, \tag{3.2}$$

$$I_b(e) = hash(e) \mod 2^{l_b}, \tag{3.3}$$

$$I'_b(e) = (I_b(e)) \mod 2^{l_b}. \tag{3.4}$$

The segment index I_s varies with expansion rounds. For a segment finished its $i+1$-th expansion round, the segment index I_s is derived with the following equation:

$$I_s(e) = (hash(e) >> l_b) \mod (2^{i+1} N_0) \tag{3.5}$$

The segment index calculation requires tracking the current expansion round. The Bamboo filter expands segments sequentially, resulting in two distinct states during the $i + 1$-th round of expansion: segments that expanded in this round and segments that expanded in the last round. Consequently, during the $i + 1$-th expansion round, the algorithm initially assumes the target segment has expanded and compute the segment index using 3.5. The validity of this premise is verified by checking whether the derived segment index falls within the current hash table capacity. If the index does not exceed the maximum index of the hash table, the segment index is derived. Otherwise, the segment index is adjusted to reflect the segment's state before the $i + 1$-th round using the following equation:

$$I_s(e) = ((hash(e) >> l_b) \mod (2^{i+1} N_0)) - 2^i N_0 \tag{3.6}$$

The insertion operation within each segment follows a Cuckoo filter-like approach. When inserting fingerprint f, the algorithm first checks the two candidate buckets for available slots. If either bucket contains an unoccupied entry, f is inserted directly. When both buckets are full, the procedure selects and evicts an existing fingerprint f' randomly to make space for f. If the alternate bucket of fingerprint f' has unoccupied entries, f' can be inserted directly. This eviction-insertion process repeats recursively until either finding an empty slot or reaching the maximum eviction threshold M_e. Upon hitting the threshold, the overflow is handled by placing the last evicted fingerprint in the segment's overflow chain. The algorithm prioritizes inserting the fingerprint into any non-overflowing segment within the existing overflow chain. If all overflow chain segments are at capacity, a new segment is appended to the chain to accommodate the fingerprint.

When an element is inserted without exceeding the iteration threshold, Bamboo filter exhibits identical time and space complexity to Cuckoo filter, characterized by constant-time operations and minimal memory overhead. In cases where a segment overflow occurs, the algorithm attempts to resolve the conflict by inserting the fingerprint into the segments within the overflow chain. The overflow chain length is bounded, guaranteeing that the incurred overhead remains asymptotically negligible. This design ensures that the time and space complexity of insertion operations maintain an amortized constant bound.

3.2.2.2 Expansion

The filter employs an automatic expansion mechanism that appends a new segment after every K element insertions, independent of overflow states. This K value serves as a critical tuning parameter—decreasing it triggers more frequent rehashing of overflow segment fingerprints. As detailed in Algorithm 11, the expansion process executes through four key phases: (1) target segment identification, (2) new segment allocation at the table's end, (3) optimized fingerprint redistribution using the i-th bit of each fingerprint as a rehashing criterion, and (4) reset of the segment split index counter to 0 upon cycle completion.

The expansion mechanism in the Bamboo filter employs a localized rehashing strategy, where each expansion operation only processes elements within a single segment. This targeted approach significantly reduces the per-operation time overhead compared to global rehashing methods. An individual expansion's time and space complexity is directly influenced by the length of the overflow chain associated with the target segment.

Algorithm 11 Append a new segment to the Bamboo filter

```
function EXPAND
    F ← the Bamboo filter requiring expansion
    p ← index of segment requiring splitting
    i ← the round of expansion
    segment[p'] is appended at the end of F for accommodating new elements
    for fingerprint f ∈ segment[p] do
        if the (i − 1)-th bit of f is 1 then
            insert f into segment[p']
        end if
    end for
    p ← p + 1
    if p equals to 2^i N_0 then
        p ← 0
    end if
end function
```

Algorithm 12 Query a key in the Bamboo filter

```
function QUERY(key e)
    calculate f, I_b, I'_b, I_s according to key e
    if f can be found in segment[I_s].bucket[I_b] or segment[I_s].bucket[I'_b] then
        return true
    end if
    if segment[I_s] has overflow segments then
        return query result from the segments in the overflow chain
    end if
    return false
end function
```

3.2.2.3 Query

The Bamboo filter's query operation, as formalized in Algorithm 12, initiates by deriving the fingerprint f, segment index I_s, and corresponding bucket indices I_b and $I_{b'}$ for the target key e. The algorithm then probes both candidate buckets within the designated segment for fingerprint f. If the fingerprint is absent, the search extends to segments in the overflow chain. A key is determined to be nonexistent if the fingerprint remains undetected. Consequently, lookup time complexity scales linearly with the overflow chain length, which can be maintained at a constant bound.

3.2.2.4 Deletion

The deletion process is outlined in Algorithm 13. It begins by calculating the fingerprint f, segment index I_s, and corresponding bucket indices I_b and $I_{b'}$ for the target key e. The algorithm then searches for matching fingerprints in both candidate buckets of segment I_s and, if necessary, traverses the overflow chain.

Algorithm 13 Delete a key in the Bamboo filter

function DELETE(key e)
  calculate f, I_b, I_b', I_s according to key e
  if f can be found in $segment[I_s].bucket[I_b]$ or $segment[I_s].bucket[I_b']$ **then**
    erase one f from the two buckets
    invoke Compress() if the compression is triggered
    return success
  end if
  if $segment[I_s]$ has overflow segments **then**
    try to erase one f from these segments
  end if
  return failure
end function

Upon finding a matching fingerprint, the operation removes one instance of it. When the compression condition is triggered, the algorithm invokes a dedicated compression operation to eliminate the final segment, thereby improving space efficiency.

The time and space complexity is the same as that of the lookup operation. Furthermore, the delete operation may trigger the compression operation, an inverse of the expansion operation.

3.2.2.5 Compression

The compression operation activates when the filter's element count falls below an integer multiple of the predetermined threshold K, maintaining memory footprint in direct proportion to current data volume rather than peak historical usage. During compression, all fingerprints in the last (most recently added) segment are rehashed and redistributed to the preceding segment in the hash table. After that, the last segment is removed from the hash table, effectively reclaiming its allocated memory. This process mirrors the reverse of the expansion operation; therefore, they have the same time and space complexity.

3.2.3 Analysis and Optimization

3.2.3.1 Optimization on Expansion and Compression Operation

While the expansion operation incurs relatively low overhead, frequent expansions during insertion operations can still degrade throughput due to the associated fingerprint redistribution and memory allocation costs. To mitigate this, three complementary strategies can be employed:

- **Adjusting the fingerprint eviction threshold M_e.** By increasing M_e, the filter allows more fingerprints to remain in their current segments before triggering eviction. This reduces the likelihood of hash collisions and delays segment overflow, thereby minimizing the need for immediate expansion.
- **Optimizing bucket size in the overflow chain.** Expanding the bucket capacity within segments of the overflow chain directly addresses the overflow of segments. Larger buckets accommodate more fingerprints without triggering overflow, reducing the pressure to expand the segment.
- **Pre-allocating initial capacity.** Increasing the filter's initial capacity ensures that early-stage insertions have ample space to avoid premature expansions. While this increases memory footprint at initialization, it avoids the performance penalties of dynamic resizing during active operations.

The compression and expansion operations in the Bamboo filter share the same threshold K, with their respective trigger conditions tied to changes in the total element count. Specifically, expansion is initiated when the element count increases by K, while compression is triggered when the count decreases by the same K. However, under mixed workloads (e.g., alternating insertions and deletions) near these transition boundaries, the system may experience frequent oscillations between expansion and compression. This phenomenon, termed churning, introduces unnecessary overhead due to repeated memory allocations and deallocations. To mitigate this issue, the trigger thresholds for expansion and compression can be decoupled by introducing asymmetric bounds. For example, expansion/compression is activated when the element count is increased by K_1/reduced by K_2, respectively. This hysteresis mechanism creates a buffer zone between expansion and compression thresholds, preventing rapid state transitions during workload fluctuations.

3.2.3.2 Theoretical Analysis

The load factor $z(n)$ for a Bamboo filter with n elements is defined as follows:

$$z(n) = \frac{n}{\alpha s N_0} \tag{3.7}$$

where N_0 denotes the initial number of segments prior to expansion, α is the target load factor per segment, and s is the capacity per segment.

The expectation of overflow chain length $E_l(n)$ for a Bamboo filter containing n elements is determined by

$$E_l(n) = x(n)l(z(n)/2) + (1 - x(n))l(z(n)), \tag{3.8}$$

where $z(n) = \frac{n}{\alpha s N_0}$, $x(n) = \frac{2\lfloor n/K \rfloor}{N_0 + \lfloor n/K \rfloor}$, $P(X = x, z) = \frac{1}{\sqrt{2\pi \alpha s z}} e^{-\frac{(x-\alpha s z)^2}{2\alpha s z}}$, $l(z) = \sum_{k=1}^{\infty} \sum_{j=1} \lfloor \alpha s \rfloor k P(\alpha s + (k-1)\alpha s + j, z)$.

The Bamboo filter, like most probabilistic filter data structures, guarantees no false negatives while retaining a bounded false positive rate (FPR). The FPR upper bound $\epsilon(z)$ is derived by

$$\epsilon(z) = 1 - \left\{1 - \frac{1}{2^{l_f - n_e}}\right\}^{\lceil 2b+2bl(z)\rceil} \approx \frac{\lceil 2b + 2bl(z)\rceil}{2^{l_f - n_e}}, \tag{3.9}$$

where b is the number of entries per bucket, $l(z) = \sum_{k=1}^{\infty}\sum_{j=1}^{\lfloor \alpha s\rfloor} kP(\alpha s+(k-1)\alpha s+j, z)$, l_f denotes the fingerprint length, n_e is the completed expansion round count, and $P(X = x, z) = \frac{1}{\sqrt{2\pi\alpha s z}}e^{-\frac{(x-\alpha s z)^2}{2\alpha s z}}$.

The space utilization $u(n)$ of a Bamboo filter with n inserted elements is modeled by

$$u(n) = \frac{n}{N(x(n)t(z(n)/2) + (1 - x(n))t(z(n)))}, \tag{3.10}$$

where N is the number of segments in the filter, $t(z) = s + \sum_{k=1}^{\infty}\sum_{j=1}^{\lfloor \alpha s\rfloor} kP(\alpha s + (k - 1)\alpha s+j, z)$, $P(X = x, z) = \frac{1}{\sqrt{2\pi\alpha s z}}e^{-\frac{(x-\alpha s z)^2}{2\alpha s z}}$, $x(n) = \frac{2\lfloor n/K\rfloor}{N_0+\lfloor n/K\rfloor}$, and $z(n) = \frac{n}{\alpha s N_0}$.

3.3 InfiniFilter

When the size of a data set cannot be known in advance, filters are required to support dynamic expansion. However, existing filter expansion methods suffer from several issues: an expansive query operation over the whole structure, a large amount of space overhead, plummeting performance in each operation, an increasing false positive rate (FPR), and finite number of expansion operations. InfiniFilter [5] is proposed to resolve these issues. It doubles its size in each expansion, and 1 bit is moved from the fingerprint to the slot address. Slots in the filter adopt a new format, such that newer entries can have longer fingerprints and the FPR can remain stable. By connecting the InfiniFilters into a chain and allowing slightly growing memory space, it can support infinite expansion operation with a stable FPR.

3.3.1 Structure: Filters in a Chain

The basic InfiniFilter is created with an array of S slots, where S is a power of 2 to ensure efficient address mapping and alignment with bitwise operations. Each slot occupies $F + 4$ bits, including 3-bit metadata. The metadata scheme is the

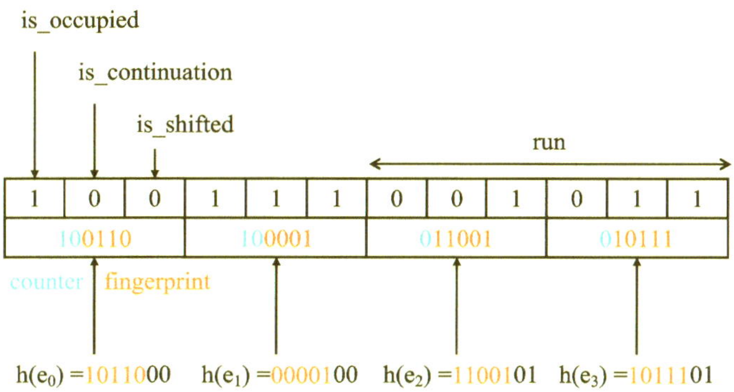

Fig. 3.6 Basic InfiniFilter structure

same as that of the Quotient filter [8]. However, the remaining bits in the slot are divided into two parts: one is the counter, and the other is the fingerprint, while in the Quotient filter, all remaining bits are used to store the fingerprints. Figure 3.6 shows an example of the basic InfiniFilter structure. In this example, the fingerprints of e_0, e_1, e_2, e_3 are inserted. The least significant 2 bits are used for selecting the index of the canonical slot. Fingerprints with the same canonical slot are formed in a run. For different types of fingerprints, different metadata bits are set. For instance, on slot 01, all three metadata bits are set because there is a run whose canonical slot is 01. In addition, the entry stored in slot 01 belongs to a run whose canonical slot is 00. The fingerprints are inserted at different expansion ages; therefore, the fingerprint lengths are different. In this example, e_0 is inserted one expansion age ago. Therefore, its counter bit is 10. During each expansion, the filter concatenates the least significant bit of the fingerprint with the canonical slot index to derive the new location for reinsertion in the expanded structure. A 1-bit flag is also appended to the most significant bit of the counter field during reinsertion. This flag serves as a temporal marker, indicating the number of expansions the element has survived. Similarly, e_2 and e_3 are inserted with one and zero expansions, respectively.

The basic InfiniFilter has a fundamental limitation that restricts its expansion capability to a finite number of operations: as the filter expands, the oldest entries eventually exhaust their allocated fingerprint bit capacity, resulting in void entries. When such void entries exist, the filter loses its ability to perform further expansions, thereby constraining scalability. To address this limitation and enable unbounded expansion, a chained InfiniFilter architecture is introduced, as illustrated in Fig. 3.7. This design employs a chain structure composed of multiple basic InfiniFilter components, enabling seamless capacity scaling while preserving operational consistency.

All insertion operations target the Active InfiniFilter, which stores new element fingerprints in its allocated slots. Upon reaching its expansion threshold α, the Active InfiniFilter initiates an expansion operation similar to the basic InfiniFilter. During expansion, void entries (the oldest entries with insufficient fingerprint bits)

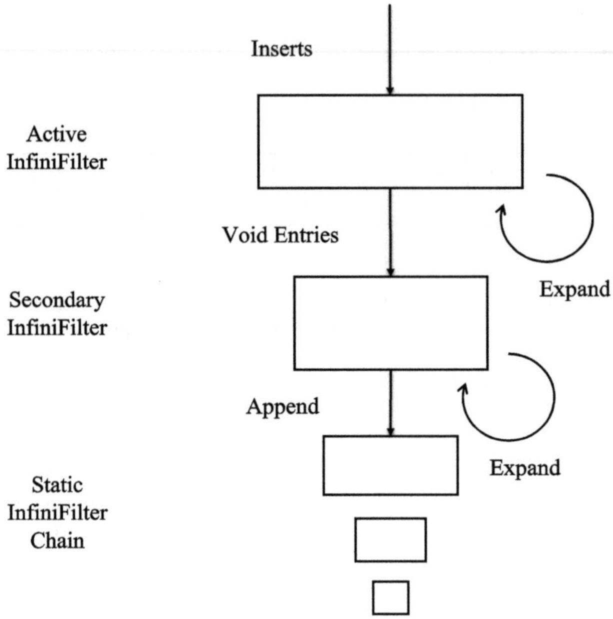

Fig. 3.7 Chained InfiniFilter structure

are migrated to a Secondary InfiniFilter in the chain. This migration clears the Active InfiniFilter of obsolete entries, enabling it to continue expanding while offloading legacy data to downstream filters.

The Secondary InfiniFilter operates on a hierarchical memory compression strategy, with its slot capacity scaled down by a factor of 2^{F+1} compared to the Active component. Upon receiving a migrated void entry, the top F bits of its canonical slot address are repurposed as the fingerprint in the Secondary component, while the remaining lower-order bits serve as the new canonical slot address. It undergoes a preliminary expansion using a process analogous to the basic InfiniFilter before expanding the Active InfiniFilter. This ensures sufficient capacity to accommodate incoming void entries. Once the Secondary InfiniFilter hits its expansion limit, its oldest entries (now void) are offloaded to a chain of static InfiniFilters, followed by the allocation of a fresh Secondary InfiniFilter to resume data inserting.

3.3.2 Operation

Both the basic InfiniFilter and the chained InfiniFilter support five operations: insertion operation, expansion operation, query operation, deletion operation, and rejuvenation operation.

3.3.2.1 Insertion

For the basic InfiniFilter, a new entry is inserted with a F bit fingerprint and an empty age counter. This age counter indicates that no expansion operation has happened since the insertion of the entry. Beyond this initialization, the insertion process follows the standard protocol of Quotient filters, including slot location and collision resolution.

For the chained InfiniFilter, the insertion operation only happens on the Active InfiniFilter. New entries are inserted directly into this component using the basic InfiniFilter's protocol. The Secondary InfiniFilter only stores the void entries from the Active InfiniFilter. The static InfiniFilter does not support insertion operations.

3.3.2.2 Expansion

The basic InfiniFilter employs a threshold-based expansion mechanism to manage capacity under dynamic workloads. When the occupancy ratio (i.e., the fraction of occupied slots) exceeds a predefined threshold α, the filter initiates an expansion operation. First, a new InfiniFilter with twice the capacity is instantiated. Then, the original InfiniFilter is iterated from the beginning to the end. The canonical slot index and the fingerprint of each entry are concatenated to get the original hash value and migrate to the new InfiniFilter. The relocation logic examines the least significant bit of the original fingerprint to determine the new canonical slot—entries with a 0 remain in their original position i, while those with a 1 move to an offset position $i + q/2$ in the expanded structure, where q represents the capacity of the new InfiniFilter. Because the former least significant bit is included in the index of the new canonical slot, the length of the new fingerprint is reduced by 1 bit. To preserve the total bit length while allowing for longer fingerprints in subsequent insertions, the age counter with 1 is padded at the most significant bit. Finally, the original InfiniFilter is deleted.

For the chained InfiniFilter, if the Active InfiniFilter reaches a particular threshold of α, it will be expanded. If there is a Secondary InfiniFilter, it will be expanded before the expansion of Active InfiniFilter. During Secondary InfiniFilter expansion, encountering a void entry initiates a transition—the current Secondary InfiniFilter converts to a static state and joins the filter chain while simultaneously spawning a fresh Secondary InfiniFilter. When expanding the Active InfiniFilter, the system offloads void entries to the Secondary InfiniFilter, automatically provisioning a new one if none exists. This layered approach ensures continuous operation by maintaining a dynamic buffer for aging data while systematically archiving void entries through the filter chain's hierarchical structure.

3.3.2.3 Query

For the basic InfiniFilter, the lookup process mirrors the quotient filter's query mechanism by first locating the target run, a continuous block of slots with identical quotient values. For every entry within this run, the operation decodes the age counter's high-order bits to reconstruct the full fingerprint and then performs a bitwise comparison with the query's fingerprint suffix. A successful match verifies the element's membership in the collection. The system returns a negative result only after exhaustively examining all entries in the identified run without finding a correspondence.

The chained InfiniFilter implements a tiered query strategy to efficiently verify membership across its components. The query first examines the Active InfiniFilter, where the most recent entries are stored. If no match is found in the Active InfiniFilter, the query proceeds to the Secondary InfiniFilter, which contains void entries from previous expansions. When neither the Active nor Secondary InfiniFilter yields a match, the query traverses the static InfiniFilter chain in chronological order (from youngest to oldest).

When a matching fingerprint is found, the process terminates and a positive result is returned. If no matching fingerprint is found, a negative result is returned. Although the query complexity is theoretically $O(log(N)/F)$ memory accesses (due to the logarithmic depth of the static chain), most positive queries can be completed after searching the Active InfiniFilter. Also, the static InfiniFilters chain is typically empty if the dataset is not that large. Therefore, most queries only access the Active InfiniFilter and the Secondary InfiniFilter.

3.3.2.4 Deletion

The basic InfiniFilter supports deletion operation, though it requires more caution to avoid false negatives and maintain correct semantics. This is due to the inherent complexity of variable-length fingerprints within a run, and directly removing a shorter fingerprint risks invalidating future queries to false negatives, as the fingerprint could match other keys. Thus, among the matching fingerprints, the longest fingerprint is selected for deletion to avoid false negatives.

Similarly, the chained InfiniFilter must remove the longest matching fingerprint. If a shorter fingerprint in a newer InfiniFilter and a longer fingerprint in an older InfiniFilter coexist in a chain, and the shorter fingerprint is deleted, a false negative could occur in future queries. Therefore, the deletion operation traverses the InfiniFilter building blocks, from largest to smallest. For each InfiniFilter, the deletion operation for the basic InfiniFilter is applied. If the longest matching fingerprint is found and removed, the procedure is terminated (note that if the counter is 0, it is the longest fingerprint in the basic InfiniFilter). Otherwise, the deletion operation is applied to the next smaller InfiniFilter. In the worst case, it needs $O(log(N)/F)$ memory accesses. However, the deletion operation typically locates and removes the target element within the Active InfiniFilter. If this removal results in a filter in the static chain becoming empty, that filter is subsequently deleted.

3.3.2.5 Rejuvenation

The InfiniFilter incorporates a rejuvenation mechanism that dynamically reduces FPR by enhancing the fingerprints of older entries during query operations. Typically, after a positive query result, the system performs a lookup in the storage to fetch the original element. This process creates an opportunity to rejuvenate (i.e., lengthen) the matched fingerprint: upon retrieving the original key, it is rehashed to generate an updated, longer fingerprint. By iteratively refining fingerprints in this manner, the system progressively optimizes its FPR, improving query accuracy over time without additional computational overhead.

However, this operation carries a risk to the correctness of the semantics. Similar to the deletion operation, if a shorter fingerprint is lengthened, false negatives may occur later, because this fingerprint may not correspond to the key. Thus, InfiniFilter ensures only the longest matching fingerprint within the run is extended. Remaining shorter fingerprints retain their validity for future queries, and the false negatives can be eliminated.

The chained InfiniFilter extends the rejuvenation mechanism to optimize FPRs across its hierarchical structure. For the Active InfiniFilter, it follows the basic InfiniFilter rejuvenation protocol. For the static components (Secondary InfiniFilter or subsequent filters), the entry with the longest matching fingerprint is migrated to the Active InfiniFilter with an extended fingerprint. This ensures that the most up-to-date and accurate fingerprint resides in the active layer. When a filter in the static chain is empty after this operation, it is deleted.

3.3.3 Analysis

3.3.3.1 Properties of the Basic InfiniFilter

The expansion threshold α in the InfiniFilter governs a critical occupancy vs. performance trade-off. A higher α (e.g., 90%) maximizes memory utilization by delaying expansions until slots are nearly full. The enhanced performance is achieved at the expense of higher operational overhead, as denser occupancy leads to extended runs of entries in the filter, thereby elevating the memory access count for insertion, query, and deletion operations. Also, the average length of collision chains grows, degrading throughput. Empirically, a threshold of $\alpha = 80\%$ strikes an optimal balance between space efficiency and operational speed.

After F expansion operations, the filter exhausts the available bits in the fingerprint used for slot mapping. Future expansion operations cannot be employed, because there are no more bits to insert an entry in the expanded filter. Hence, the maximum expansion count of a basic InfiniFilter is F, resulting in a maximum capacity of $S \cdot 2^F$. With a chained InfiniFilter structure, the expansion operation can be employed indefinitely.

The InfiniFilter's doubling expansion strategy inherently creates an exponentially decaying age distribution of entries. For each expansion, the number of entries with age $i + 1$ is approximately half that of entries with age i, yielding the post-X-expansion age distribution as follows:

$$f(i) \lesssim 2^{-i-1} \qquad 0 \leq i \leq X \tag{3.11}$$

Age-i entries maintain $F - i$ bit-resolution fingerprints, exhibiting cohort-specific false positive probability $2^{-F+i} \cdot \alpha$. The composite FPR emerges as:

$$\begin{aligned} \theta = \sum_{i=0}^{X} f(i) \cdot 2^{-F+i} \cdot \alpha &\lesssim (X+2) \cdot 2^{-F-1} \cdot \alpha \\ &\lesssim (F+2) \cdot 2^{-F-1} \cdot \alpha \end{aligned} \tag{3.12}$$

As illustrated in Eq. 3.12, the FPR exhibits a linear relationship with the number of expansions X. Given the doubling expansion strategy, this manifests as logarithmic FPR growth relative to dataset cardinality. Although older entries become exponentially fewer in number (as shown in Eq. 3.11), they simultaneously contribute exponentially higher FPR. This balance ensures that each epoch produce equipartitioned FPR contributions. The FPR attains its supremum after F expansions, as the system can only support up to F expansions before the fingerprint length is exhausted.

3.3.3.2 Properties of the Chained InfiniFilter

After the initial F expansions, the system maintains entries distributed across $F+1$ consecutive epochs in both the Active InfiniFilter and subsequent filters in the chain. The total expansion count X given by $\lceil log_2(N) + 1 \rceil$. Therefore, the total number of InfiniFilters is $c = \lceil (log_2(N) + 1)/(F + 1) \rceil$.

The chained InfiniFilter's false positive behavior emerges from its hierarchical structure—each constituent filter can independently generate false positives during membership queries. This architectural characteristic leads to an aggregate false positive probability that combines contributions from all filters in the chain. Equation 3.13 captures this relationship and approximates the FPR θ with a smooth function. The FPR grows logarithmically with the number of elements N.

$$\theta \lesssim (log_2(N) + 2) \cdot 2^{-F-1} \cdot \alpha \tag{3.13}$$

3.3.3.3 Stabilizing the FPR

InfiniFilter's rejuvenation mechanism mitigates false positives by adaptively increasing fingerprint precision for accessed items. This strategy's efficacy, however, depends critically on query distribution: when queries concentrate on a limited key subset, dormant entries retain their initial short fingerprints. Consequently, collision risks persist for older entries encoded with lower bit-resolution, constraining overall false positive reduction.

The chained InfiniFilter variant fundamentally improves worst-case false positive guarantees. Its Active component progressively widens slots during scale-up, assigning newer entries longer fingerprints. This precision escalation for recent inserts directly offsets collision vulnerability from legacy entries' truncated representations. By dynamically calibrating fingerprint resolution across temporal cohorts, the architecture sustains a stable, suppressed false positive rate even under skewed query workloads.

InfiniFilter orchestrates stable false positive rates through multiple expansions via adaptive fingerprint precision scaling. This is achieved through a gradual, controlled growth of fingerprint lengths, where the incremental increase is carefully balanced to avoid excessive memory overhead. The key to this balance lies in the use of a convergent mathematical series: the reciprocal of square numbers $\left(\sum_{i=0}^{\infty} i^{-2} = \pi^2/6\right)$. For entries inserted after the Xth expansions, slot-width escalation enables FPR suppression by a $(X+1)^{-2}$ factor. The resultant fingerprint length for such entries, denoted in Eq. 3.14, scales from baseline length F as:

$$\ell(X) = F + \lceil 2 \cdot log_2(X+1) \rceil \tag{3.14}$$

The chained InfiniFilter's FPR is derived through fingerprint length analysis across temporal cohorts. For a filter instantiated at epoch t (post-t expansions), its operational lifespan spans $\ell(t)$ consecutive insertion epochs before the oldest entries expire. Within this construct, entries inserted at epoch $t+i$ originate with $\ell(t+i)$-bit fingerprints. Prior to appendint to the chain, $\ell(t) - i$ subsequent expansions occur, reducing these fingerprints by $\ell(t) - i$ bits due to slot addressing requirements. The effective fingerprint length for epoch-$t+i$ entries in an epoch-t filter is formalized in Eq. 3.15:

$$FP_t(i) = \ell(t+i) - (\ell(t) - i) = F + 2 \cdot log_2(t+i+1) - \ell(t) + i \tag{3.15}$$

The FPR θ_t of an InfiniFilter created at epoch t (Eq. 3.16) synthesizes generational collision probabilities weighted by temporal distribution (Eq. 3.11):

$$\theta_t = \sum_{i=0}^{\ell(t)} f(\ell(t) - i) \cdot 2^{-FP_t(i)} \cdot \alpha \lesssim 2^{-F-1} \cdot \alpha \sum_{i=1}^{\ell(t)+1} \frac{1}{(t+i)^2} \tag{3.16}$$

The overall FPR θ (Eq. 3.17) emerges from basic filter chaining, exhibiting asymptotic stabilization independent of expansion count:

$$\begin{aligned}\theta \leq 2^{-F-1} \cdot \alpha \sum_{i=1}^{X+1} \frac{1}{i^2} &\lesssim 2^{-F-1} \cdot \alpha \sum_{i=0}^{\infty} \frac{1}{i^2} \\ &= 2^{-F-1} \cdot \alpha \cdot \frac{\pi^2}{6} \lesssim 2^{-F-1} \cdot \alpha\end{aligned} \tag{3.17}$$

3.4 Variable-Length Encoding Framework

The dynamic nature of modern data processing necessitates filter structures that can adapt to fluctuating workload sizes while ensuring space efficiency. However, conventional filters often store fixed-bit representations for inserted keys, resulting in inefficient space allocation when occupancy rates fall below capacity thresholds. For instance, Cuckoo filter employs a fixed-length fingerprint for each key. When the filter contains only a few elements, allocated space significantly exceeds actual requirements, creating underutilized storage regions.

The Variable-Length Encoding Framework (VLE Framework) [6] offers a solution to this issue through its innovative encoding length adaptation. By dynamically adjusting the bit length per key based on occupancy levels, this framework leverages the unused space to maintain a lower false positive rate (FPR). The framework's generic design allows it to integrate with various filter architectures, including but not limited to Cuckoo-based and Bloom-based filters.

3.4.1 *Structure: Filters with Variable-Length Encoding*

The VLE Framework demonstrates broad applicability across diverse filter architectures by categorizing existing filters into two distinct storage paradigms: gather approach-based filters and scatter approach-based filters. As illustrated in Fig. 3.8,

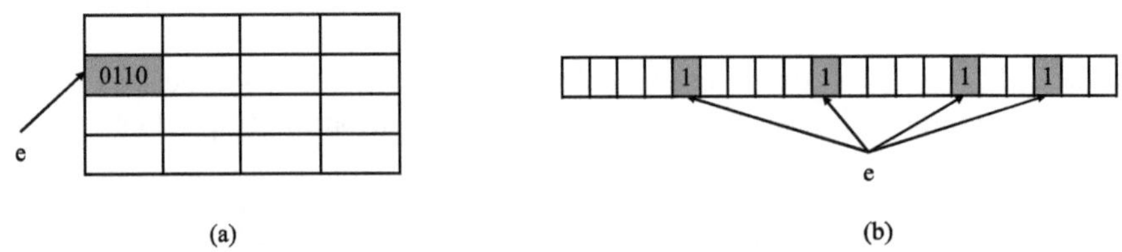

Fig. 3.8 Example of inserting element e with different types of filters. (**a**) Gathered approach-based filter. (**b**) Scattered approach-based filter

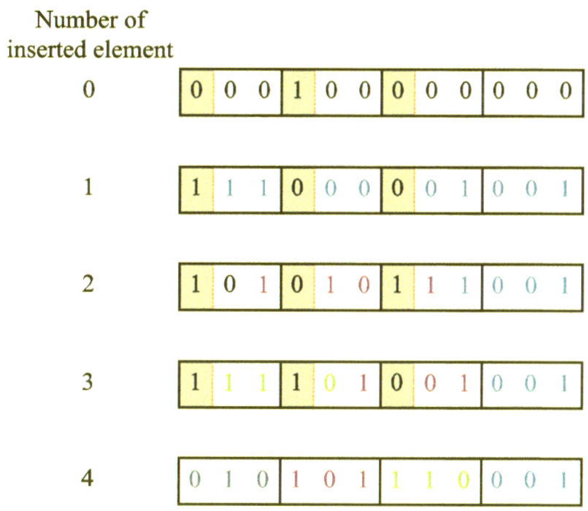

Fig. 3.9 An example of the bucket structures of gathered approach-based filters, with different numbers of inserted elements

the storage scheme of an element e exhibits fundamentally different mechanisms depending on the filter type. Gathered approach-based filters (such as derivatives of Cuckoo filters) operate by encoding each element into a compact fingerprint and storing these compressed representations in contiguous memory regions. In contrast, the scattered approach-based filters (such as derivatives of Bloom filters) map each element to dispersed memory addresses through independent hash functions. The architectural divergence between these two paradigms necessitates tailored adaptations of the VLE Framework.

Gathered approach-based filters utilize a three-tiered hierarchical storage architecture: hash tables, buckets, and slots. The top-level hash table partitions the data into multiple buckets, and each bucket is equipped with b slots. Every slot stores a compact, fixed-size fingerprint of l_f bits. However, this rigid structure leads to inefficiencies when a bucket contains fewer fingerprints than its capacity. Unused slots remain, resulting in suboptimal space utilization.

The VLE Framework addresses this issue by redefining the slot allocation strategy. Through its adaptive encoding mechanism, the framework ensures full utilization of all slots even when only one fingerprint is stored in a bucket. Therefore, the FPR is optimized. As illustrated in Fig. 3.9, the bucket structures adapt dynamically to varying insertion counts. For clarity, the example uses four slots per bucket—a common configuration in Cuckoo-based filters. While the framework supports buckets with arbitrary slot counts, this simplified representation highlights the core principles of space-efficient encoding. In this example, the highest bit of the first three buckets serves as a bucket type identifier to distinguish between different occupancy states.

- When the bucket contains fewer fingerprints than its capacity (four slots in this example), the framework deliberately avoids monotonic ordering of the first three buckets by setting these bits to nonsequential patterns (e.g., 010, 100, 101, 110). The remaining bits are equally divided for each fingerprint.

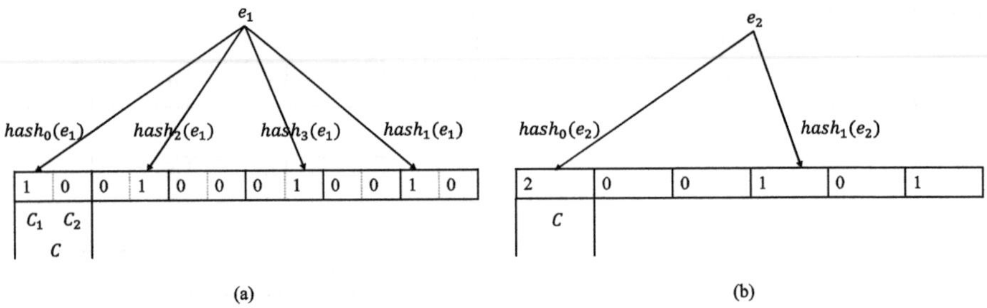

Fig. 3.10 An example of the slot structures in Counting Bloom filter. (**a**) A Bloom filter with $k' = 4$ hash functions. (**b**) A Bloom filter with $k = 2$ hash functions

- When the bucket is fully occupied (four fingerprints), fingerprints in the first three buckets follow an ascending order, creating distinct identifiers that avoid conflicts with partial-occupancy cases.

Scattered approach-based filters, such as Bloom filters and their variants, rely on hash distribution mechanisms to map elements to multiple memory positions. During insertion, k distinct hash functions compute k storage indices in the array for each element. The VLE Framework enhances this design by dynamically adjusting how many hash functions are used according to the current occupancy level. Specifically, for a filter with capacity N: when the element count is lower than $\alpha \cdot N (0 < \alpha < 1)$, k' hash functions are used ($k' > k$); otherwise, k hash functions are used.

As illustrated in Fig. 3.10, this adaptation is demonstrated using a Counting Bloom filter. When k' hash functions are active, the slot C is divided into into two subregions: C_1 and C_2. C_1 stores the information produced by the first k hash functions, while C_2 stores the information produced by the remaining $k' - k$ hash functions. In Fig. 3.10a, when inserting e_1, $hash_0(e_1)$ and $hash_1(e_1)$ are updated on C_1, $hash_2(e_1)$ and $hash_3(e_1)$ are updated on C_2. However, once the element count surpasses $\alpha \cdot N$, C_2 is cleared, C_1 and C_2 are merged as C, and following operations only use k hash functions. In Fig. 3.10b, when inserting e_2, $hash_0(e_2)$ and $hash_1(e_2)$ are updated on C.

3.4.2 Operation

Filters with the VLE Framework support three operations: insertion operation, query operation, and deletion operation. Cuckoo filters and the Counting Bloom filter are taken as examples to illustrate how to apply the framework to the gathered approach-based filters and scattered approach-based filters, respectively. However, the framework is orthogonal to underlying filters, since their original insertion, query, and deletion mechanisms are preserved. Because of this nonintrusive design, the framework can be easily integrated with other existing filters.

3.4.2.1 Insertion

For Cuckoo filter, each element e is associated with two candidate buckets i_1 and i_2. Given the fingerprint bit-length l_f, f, i_1 and i_2 can be calculated as follows:

$$f = fingerprint(e) \mod 2^{l_f} \tag{3.18}$$

$$i_1 = hash(e); i_2 = i_1 \oplus hash(f) \tag{3.19}$$

The integration of the VLE Framework introduces a crucial architectural consideration: preserving bucket index consistency while accommodating dynamic fingerprint length adaptation. To achieve this, the framework employs a fixed-bit hashing strategy: the lower l_f bits of the variable-length fingerprint are consistently used to compute the two candidate bucket indexes i_1 and i_2. For an element e with a variable-length fingerprint f' (of bit-length $l_{f'}$), the computational process unfolds as follows:

$$f' = fingerprint(e) \mod 2^{l_{f'}} \tag{3.20}$$

$$i_1 = hash(e); i_2 = i_1 \oplus hash(f \mod 2^{l_f}) \tag{3.21}$$

The insertion operation in the Cuckoo filter enhanced by the VLE Framework maintains full compatibility with the original Cuckoo filter in the bucket-level mechanism. The algorithm first examines both candidate buckets and inserts the variable-length fingerprint f' into one of the candidates if either bucket contains available slots, updating its internal structure accordingly. When both buckets are full, a random existing fingerprint f'' is selected for eviction. The evicted f'' is redirected to its alternate bucket using the standard Cuckoo hashing scheme. If this bucket has space, f'' is placed there, and the process terminates successfully. Otherwise, another displacement is triggered recursively, propagating the chain until a valid placement is found or a predefined threshold is exceeded.

The Counting Bloom filter utilizes a memory array C of length m, where each slot is a c-bit counter initialized to zero. During insertion operations, the framework computes k hash functions and increments the corresponding counters according to the input key e, following the update rule defined in Eq. 3.22:

$$C[hash_i(e)] = C[hash_i(e)] + 1, i \in [0, k) \tag{3.22}$$

The integration of the VLE Framework introduces a two-phase insertion mechanism that adapts to varying occupancy levels. The operation proceeds as follows:

1. When the element count is lower than $\alpha \cdot N$, the framework partitions each c-bit counter into two $c/2$-bit sub-counters, denoted as C_1 and C_2. The C_1 counter stores the information generated by the first k hash functions. The C_2 counter stores the additional information generated by the remaining $k' - k$ hash functions. Therefore, the value of k C_1 counters and $k' - k$ C_2 counters are

updated according to Eq. 3.23:

$$C_1[hash_i(e)] = C_1[hash_i(e)] + 1, i \in [0, k) \tag{3.23}$$

$$C_2[hash_i(e)] = C_2[hash_i(e)] + 1, i \in [k, k') \tag{3.24}$$

2. When the element count exceeds $\alpha \cdot N$, the framework transitions to a consolidated mode to accommodate increased demand. At this phase, the additional encoding information in C_2 counters is cleared. The C_1 and C_2 sub-counters are merged as C to accommodate further inserts. Therefore, the value of k C counters is updated according to Eq. 3.25. This irreversible transition ensures that the Counting Bloom filter operates at full capacity under high load. However, it also means the extended encoding information stored in C_2 is permanently discarded, and the filter's accuracy cannot be further improved:

$$C[hash_i(e)] = C[hash_i(e)] + 1, i \in [0, k) \tag{3.25}$$

3.4.2.2 Query

The VLE-enhanced Cuckoo filter maintains query semantics consistent with standard Cuckoo filters while supporting variable-length fingerprints. For a query element e, the process first computes its two candidate bucket indices i_1 and i_2 using the addressing scheme defined in Eq. 3.20. The system then examines both target buckets sequentially, decoding their variable-length fingerprint entries to identify any match with e's fingerprint. A successful match in either bucket confirms the membership, while absence in both buckets provides definitive nonexistence proof.

The query operation of Counting Bloom filter enhanced by the VLE Framework can be divided into two phases:

1. When the element count is lower than $\alpha \cdot N$, the existence of an element e determined by verifying nonzero values in k C_1 counters and $k' - k$ C_2 counters.
2. When the element count exceeds the threshold, the query process simplifies to checking only the k primary counters C, where the presence of nonzero values in all corresponding counters indicates element existence.

3.4.2.3 Deletion

The deletion operation of Cuckoo filters enhanced by the VLE Framework goes through a query operation. When there are matching fingerprints in the candidate buckets, the longest matching fingerprint is deleted. Similar to InfiniFilter [5], it is because removing a shorter fingerprint corresponding to the wrong key could lead to false negatives later on.

The deletion operation of the Counting Bloom filter enhanced by the VLE Framework can be divided into two phases:

1. When the element count is lower than $\alpha \cdot N$, the values of corresponding k C_1 counters and $k' - k$ C_2 counters are decremented by 1.
2. When the element count exceeds the threshold, the values of the corresponding k C counters are decremented by 1.

3.4.3 Theoretical Properties

3.4.3.1 Gathered Approach-Based Filters

The Cuckoo filter serves as an illustrative case study for VLE Framework's FPR enhancement on gathered approach-based filters. After inserting n elements, the FPR is characterized by

$$\epsilon = 2\sum_{s=1}^{b} P(X = s)\frac{s}{2^{l_s}} \tag{3.26}$$

where b is the slot capacity per bucket, s denotes stored elements in bucket, l_s represents the adaptive fingerprint length at occupancy s, $P(X = s) = \begin{cases} e^{\lambda}\lambda^s/s, & s < b, \\ 1 - \sum_{s=0}^{b-1} P(X = s), & s = b, \end{cases}$ is the occupancy distribution in the bucket, $\lambda = n/m$ denotes the filter load factor, and m represents the number of bucket.

3.4.3.2 Scattered Approach-Based Filters

The Counting Bloom filter serves as an illustrative case study for VLE Framework's FPR improvement on scattered approach-based filters. The VLE-enhanced Counting Bloom filter demonstrates significant improvements in FPR through its two-phase operation, as captured by the following piecewise model:

$$\epsilon = \begin{cases} (1 - e^{-k_1 n/m})^{k_1}, & 0 \le n \le \alpha N, \\ (1 - e^{-k_2 n/m})^{k_2}, & n > \alpha N, \end{cases} \tag{3.27}$$

where $k_1 = \frac{m}{\alpha N} ln2$ is the hash function count in the first phase, $k_2 = \frac{m}{N} ln2$ is the hash function count in the second phase, N is the filter capacity, m is the number of counters, and α is the phase transition threshold ($n > \alpha \cdot N$ triggers the second phase).

The average FPR is $\frac{1}{n}\sum_{i=0}^{n} \epsilon(i)$, with $\alpha = 0.5$ in experiments optimized for minimal FPR.

3.5 Summary and Comparision

3.5.1 Summary of Space-Resilient Filters

- **Logarithmic Dynamic Cuckoo Filter** (LDCF) [3] arranges multiple Cuckoo filters in a binary tree structure, converting expansion/compaction operations into leaf node splitting and merging. This design achieves logarithmic time complexity for query operations.
- **Bamboo filter** [4] organizes multiple Cuckoo filters in a linear array structure, transforming capacity expansion/compaction operations into tail insertions and deletions within the array. This architecture achieves constant-time complexity for query operations.
- **InfiniFilter** [5] addresses the limitation of finite fingerprint length constraining filter expansion capacity by proposing a chained architecture. This design supports unbounded expansion while maintaining a stable false positive rate.
- **Variable-Length Encoding Framework** (VLE Framework) [6] tackles the issue of space waste caused by fixed-length element encoding in filters. By introducing an adaptive encoding adjustment scheme, it enhances storage efficiency while further reducing the false positive rate.

3.5.2 Comparison of Space-Resilient Filters

Table 3.1 gives a comparison among the filters. The first three filters focus on addressing capacity scaling challenges in dynamic data scenarios, while the last filter tackles the space inefficiency caused by fixed-length element encoding when the capacity is the maximum of the dynamic dataset size. LDCF reduces the number of filters accessed during operations from linear complexity to logarithmic complexity by restructuring multiple Cuckoo filters into a hierarchical tree structure. Bamboo filter further optimizes this to constant complexity by adopting a segmented storage architecture with hash tables and segments, organizing multiple Cuckoo filters into a linear array. InfiniFilter tackles the limitation of finite fingerprint lengths that restrict infinite scalability, combining chained structures to enable

Table 3.1 Comparison of space-resilient filters. d, tree depth of LDCF; l, chain length in InfiniFilter, –, determined by underlying filter

Filter	Expandable	Infinite expanding	Variable-length encoding	Arrange structure	Query complexity
LDCF	✓	✗	✗	Tree	$O(\log d)$
Bamboo filter	✓	✗	✗	Hash table	$O(1)$
InfiniFilter	✓	✓	✗	Chain	$O(l)$
VLE Framework	–	–	✓	–	–

theoretically unbounded expansion. The fourth filter, Variable-Length Encoding Framework, addresses space waste caused by fixed-bit representations for inserted keys. It dynamically adjusts encoding schemes within filters to enhance space utilization efficiency. As a general framework, other properties are determined by the underlying filter.

3.5.3 Conclusion

This chapter focuses on introducing filters that adaptively adjust their structure to achieve space resilience in dynamic workloads. It provides an in-depth analysis of several representative works in this field, including LDCF [3], Bamboo filter [4], InfiniFilter [5], and VLE Framework [6]. These works have made significant contributions in optimizing performance, improving functionality, and utilizing space.

References

1. Singh, A., Garg, S., Kaur, K., et al.: Fuzzy-folded bloom filter-as-a-service for big data storage in the cloud. IEEE Trans. Ind. Informat. 2338–2348 (2019). https://doi.org/10.1109/TII.2018.2850053
2. Li, P., Luo, B., Zhu, W., et al.: Cluster-based distributed dynamic cuckoo filter system for redis. Int. J. Parallel Emergent Distrib. Syst. 340–353 (2020). https://doi.org/10.1080/17445760.2019.1599889
3. Zhang, F., Chen, H.H., Jin, H., et al.: The logarithmic dynamic cuckoo filter. In: 37th IEEE International Conference on Data Engineering, pp. 948–959 (2021). https://doi.org/10.1109/ICDE51399.2021.00087
4. Wang, H.C., Dai, H.P., Chen, S.S., et al.: Bamboo filters: Make resizing smooth and adaptive. IEEE/ACM Trans. Netw. 3776–3791 (2024). https://doi.org/10.1109/TNET.2024.3403997
5. Dayan, N., Bercea, I., Reviriego, P., et al.: InfiniFilter: Expanding filters to infinity and beyond. Proc. ACM Manag. Data **140**(27), 1–140 (2023). https://doi.org/10.1145/3589285
6. Dai, H.P., Wang, H.C., Chen, Z.P., et al.: Variable-length encoding framework: A generic framework for enhancing the accuracy of approximate membership queries. In: IEEE International Conference on Data Mining, pp. 61–70 (2023). https://doi.org/10.1109/ICDM58522.2023.00015
7. Chen, H.H., Liao, L.Y., Jin, H., et al.: The dynamic cuckoo filter. In: 25th IEEE International Conference on Network Protocols, pp. 1–10 (2017). https://doi.org/10.1109/ICNP.2017.8117563
8. Bender, M.A., Farach-Colton, M., Johnson, R.: Don't thrash: How to cache your hash on flash. Proc. VLDB Endow. 1627–1637 (2012). https://doi.org/10.14778/2350229.2350275

Chapter 4
Streaming Filters

Abstract In stream data processing, identifying whether an element has appeared before is a key challenge, particularly in real-time applications such as network monitoring and recommendation systems. To address storage and latency limitations, streaming filters serve as approximate membership structures, sacrificing some accuracy for space and speed while allowing false positives and false negatives. This chapter presents three notable streaming filters, each excelling in stability, space efficiency, and window flexibility.

Keywords Streaming filters · Stream processing

In stream data processing, a key goal is to determine whether an item under analysis has appeared previously in the data sequence. This challenge is highly relevant in fields like network traffic monitoring and personalized recommendation systems. Due to the massive data volumes and the need for real-time processing, traditional databases are impractical for storing stream data and checking element existence.

Streaming filters have emerged as a solution in this context, enabling the approximation of whether an element in a data stream has appeared before while using minimal space. This approximation introduces the possibility of errors. Unlike simple filter structures, which only produce false positives, streaming filters may result in both false positives and false negatives. Despite this, they offer key advantages, including low space requirements and high processing speed. Moreover, with appropriate configurations, they can achieve a low error rate, making them highly practical for real-world applications.

In this chapter, we present three typical streaming filters, each possessing distinct characteristics. First, the Stable Bloom filter (SBF) [1] is a classic representative work. It inherits from the conventional Bloom filter (BF) [2], which features a concise and effective design that lays the foundation for future research. Next, the Stable Learned Bloom filter (SLBF) [3] pioneers the integration of the recently emerged learned index concept into the field of streaming filters, thereby further reducing the space overhead required for streaming filters. Lastly, the Learned Cuckoo filter (LCF) [4] observes that the aforementioned methods only maintain a

H. Dai et al., *Advanced Filter Structure Handbook*,
https://doi.org/10.1007/978-981-95-1715-2_4

fixed-capacity window of the most recent entries in the data stream, which restricts flexibility. Consequently, based on the Cuckoo filter (CF) [5], it is a streaming filter with a variable window size, enhancing the practicality. We now proceed to introduce these three filters in sequence, covering their structural design, specific operations, and theoretical analysis.

4.1 Stable Bloom Filter (SBF)

Stable Bloom filter (SBF) [1] enhances the conventional BF [2] to suit the field of data stream processing, providing an approximate determination of whether the current element in the data stream has been encountered before. Suppose that the original BF is employed to process the data stream and continuous data insertion occurs. In that case, the density of unset bits within the BF gradually decreases and ultimately vanishes. At this juncture, any query will erroneously indicate that an element exists, rendering the BF ineffective.

To address this limitation, SBF replaces each single-bit entry in the standard BF with a multi-bits counter. When processing each element in the data stream, SBF removes some information to accommodate new elements.

4.1.1 Structure: Integer Counter Array

The structure of SBF comprises an integer array consisting of m integer counters, each occupying d bits. Consequently, the value range of each counter spans from 0 to $\mathrm{Max} = 2^d - 1$. It is evident that the structural enhancement of SBF over BF lies in the substitution of each bit in BF with a multi-bit integer counter.

4.1.2 Operations: Hashing, Counting, and Decrementing

Upon initialization of a new SBF, the integer value at each position is set to 0. For a new element arriving in the data stream, SBF employs hash functions to determine K independent and randomly distributed positions associated with the element and examines the counters at those positions within the SBF. If all these counters are nonzero, it suggests that the element exists and has been present in the preceding data stream. Conversely, if at least one of these counters is 0, it implies that the element does not exist and has not been observed in the preceding data stream.

Following the determination, SBF undertakes the operations of information removal and element insertion. It randomly selects P positions and examines the counters at these positions within the SBF. If a counter's value exceeds 0, it decrements the counter by 1. Subsequently, SBF sets the counters at the K

Algorithm 14 Approximate detection of stream element repetitions using SBF

Input: A data stream $S = x_1, x_2, \ldots, x_N$
Output: A series of binary responses indicate whether each element is a duplicate
Reset all counters in the SBF array to 0: $SBF[1 \ldots m] \leftarrow 0$
for each element $x_i \in S$ **do**
    Probe K counters: $SBF[h_1(x_i)], \ldots, SBF[h_K(x_i)]$
    if none of these K counters equals zero **then**
        $DuplicateFlag \leftarrow$ "Yes" ▷ Element is considered duplicate
    else
        $DuplicateFlag \leftarrow$ "No" ▷ Element is considered distinct
    end if
    Randomly select P distinct counters $\{j_1, \ldots, j_P\} \subseteq \{1, \ldots, m\}$
    for each selected counter $j \in \{j_1, \ldots, j_P\}$ **do**
        if $SBF[j] \geq 1$ **then**
            Decrement $SBF[j]$ by 1
        end if
    end for
    for each probed counter $c \in \{h_1(x_i), \ldots, h_K(x_i)\}$ **do**
        Set $SBF[c] \leftarrow$ Max
    end for
    Output $DuplicateFlag$
end for

positions corresponding to the current element being processed to MAX, thereby achieving the insertion of the current element. The detailed algorithm is described in Algorithm 14.

To illustrate this process concretely, consider an SBF with $m = 16$ counters, each of $d = 3$ bits (i.e., Max $= 7$), and let $K = 2$ hash functions and $P = 3$ decrement positions. Suppose we process an element A, which hashes to positions 5 and 12. Initially, both counters are 0, indicating that A is likely new. Next, SBF randomly selects three counters—say, positions 2, 7, and 14—for potential decrement. Since these counters are also 0, no decrement occurs. Finally, SBF sets the values at positions 5 and 12 to Max (7). Now, if another A arrives later, those two counters will still be nonzero (unless decremented in the meantime), correctly signaling its presence.

4.1.3 Analysis: Stability, Error Rates, and Time Complexity

4.1.3.1 Stable Property and Stable Point

SBF exhibits a stable property, which means that after a certain number of data stream elements have been processed, the proportion of counters set to 0 will gradually stabilize. Unlike the original BF, which becomes ineffective as more elements are added, the SBF maintains a consistent proportion of counters set to 0.

Furthermore, SBF has a stable point, which refers to the lower bound of the proportion of counters that remain zero after SBF reaches a steady state. The stable point of SBF is calculated by

$$\left(\frac{1}{1+\frac{1}{P\left(\frac{1}{K}-\frac{1}{m}\right)}}\right)^{\text{Max}}. \tag{4.1}$$

4.1.3.2 False Positive Rates

In streaming filters, there are two types of errors: false positives (FP) and false negatives (FN). FP occurs when an element that does not exist is erroneously judged to be present, while FN occurs when an element that does exist is erroneously judged to be absent. The probabilities of these misjudgments are referred to as the false positive rate (FPR) and false negative rate (FNR), respectively. Notably, conventional filter data structures typically only have FP without FN. FP is unique to streaming filters.

When SBF reaches stability, the upper bound of its FPR is

$$FPS = \left(1-\left(\frac{1}{1+\frac{1}{P(1/K-1/m)}}\right)^{\text{Max}}\right)^{K}. \tag{4.2}$$

This upper bound is achieved when the stream elements are uniformly distributed.

4.1.3.3 False Negative Rates

FN arises when a repeated element is mistakenly treated as new. This kind of error exclusively stems from repeated values and is heavily influenced by how input elements are spaced—specifically, the so-called gaps between a duplicate and its nearest earlier occurrence. Formally, δ_i denotes the number of elements separating a repeated item x_i and its most recent previous instance $x_{i-\delta_i}$, such $x_i = x_{i-\delta_i}$.

When such a repeated element x_i appears, it is mapped to K distinct positions in the SBF, labeled $SBF[C_{i1}], \ldots, SBF[C_{iK}]$. A false negative is triggered if any of these K counters has been reduced to zero during the δ_i updates leading up to the appearance of x_i. We denote the probability that a given counter C_{ij} reaches zero over δ_i rounds as $PR0(\delta_i, k_{ij})$, where k_{ij} is the chance that C_{ij} is set to `Max` in any given update.

This probability can be expressed as

$$\begin{aligned}\mathrm{PR0}(\delta_i, k_{ij}) = &\sum_{l=\mathrm{Max}}^{\delta_i-1} \left[\Pr(SBF_{\delta_i} = 0 \mid A_l) \cdot \Pr(A_l)\right] \\ &+ \Pr(SBF_{\delta_i} = 0 \mid \bar{A}_{\delta_i}) \cdot \Pr(\bar{A}_{\delta_i}),\end{aligned} \tag{4.3}$$

where the terms are defined as follows:

$$\Pr(SBF_{\delta_i} = 0 \mid A_l) = \sum_{j=\mathrm{Max}}^{l} \binom{l}{j} p^j (1-p)^{l-j}, \tag{4.4}$$

$$\Pr(A_l) = (1-k_{ij})^l \cdot k_{ij}, \tag{4.5}$$

$$\Pr(SBF_{\delta_i} = 0 \mid \bar{A}_{\delta_i}) = \sum_{j=\mathrm{Max}}^{\delta_i} \binom{\delta_i}{j} p^j (1-p)^{\delta_i-j}, \tag{4.6}$$

$$\Pr(\bar{A}_{\delta_i}) = (1-k_{ij})^{\delta_i}. \tag{4.7}$$

Given these definitions, the probability that a false negative occurs when x_i arrives is given by

$$\Pr(FN_i) = 1 - \prod_{j=1}^{K} \left(1 - PR0(\delta_i, k_{ij})\right). \tag{4.8}$$

It is important to note that if $\delta_i < \mathrm{Max}$, the counter reset probability $PR0(\delta_i, k_{ij})$ becomes zero, and thus no false negatives can occur in this case. Similarly, if the element is unique and has no earlier occurrence, it cannot be misclassified as a duplicate, leading to an FN probability of zero. The value of δ_i itself is dictated by how the stream is distributed.

4.1.3.4 Time Complexity

During each iteration, the algorithm begins by inspecting K cells to check if the current element is already present. Next, it chooses P cells randomly and decreases their counters by one. Finally, it sets the counters of all initially checked K cells to their maximum value. Consequently, the processing time per element depends mainly on the fixed parameters K and P. Given that K, P, and Max are all constants, the algorithm guarantees a constant time complexity of $O(1)$ for each element, regardless of the data stream length or available space.

4.2 Stable Learned Bloom Filter (SLBF)

Stable Learned Bloom filter (SLBF) [3] builds upon the foundational idea of the Learned Bloom filter (LBF) [6], which integrates learned models into traditional approximate membership testing. LBF employs a predictive model trained to distinguish between elements that belong to a set and those that do not. When a query is made, the model first estimates its likelihood of being in the set. If the confidence exceeds a predefined threshold, the element is accepted directly; otherwise, a backup BF is consulted to determine the final outcome. This hybrid design enables more compact representations by reducing reliance on the backup filter.

However, existing LBF structures are designed under the assumption of a static member set. Their performance deteriorates significantly when applied to dynamic environments involving frequent insertions or updates, which are typical in practical streaming scenarios such as event logging, content deduplication, and real-time traffic analysis.

To address this limitation and enable effective operation in streaming scenarios, SLBF is specifically designed to maintain stable performance in the presence of continuous data insertions by combining the learned model with updatable backup filters. It preserves the space efficiency of LBF while enhancing adaptability to evolving data distributions.

4.2.1 Structure: Single and Grouping SLBF

4.2.1.1 Single SLBF

To extend the original LBF for scenarios involving a potentially infinite stream of insertions, one effective strategy is to substitute the conventional backup filter—a standard BF—with a SBF capable of handling continuous updates without significant degradation. This redesigned architecture is termed a single SLBF (s-SLBF), where the term single emphasizes the presence of a lone backup component in the system (Fig. 4.1).

This structure can be formalized as a triple (f, τ, SBF), where f represents a pre-trained classification model serving as a probabilistic oracle, τ is a tunable threshold that governs the model's acceptance behavior, and SBF denotes the stable Bloom filter used as a safety net to correct potential misclassifications from the learned component.

4.2.1.2 Grouping SLBF

While the s-SLBF extends the original LBF design and can, in some cases, outperform standard stable Bloom filters in terms of space efficiency, it suffers from a

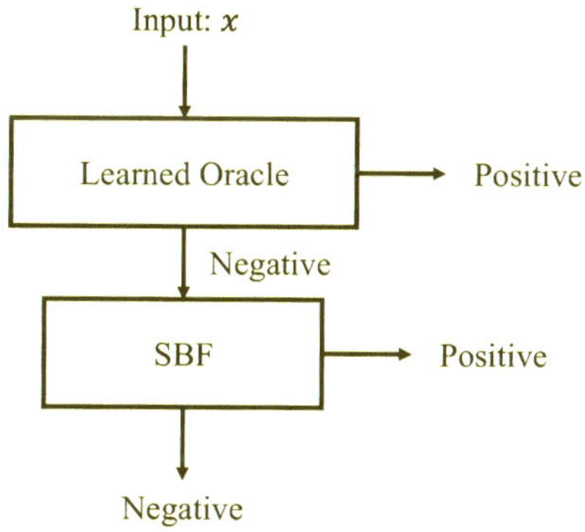

Fig. 4.1 Illustration of s-SLBF

critical inherited limitation: its blind reliance on the classifier's positive predictions. This overdependence becomes a major vulnerability when the classifier's accuracy deteriorates, such as under distribution shift or model drift. Furthermore, the use of a single backup filter in s-SLBF fails to leverage the finer-grained information embedded in the classifier's output scores.

At the core of this limitation lies the monolithic backup design shared by both LBF and s-SLBF. To address this, a more flexible architecture called the grouping SLBF (g-SLBF) is introduced. The central idea is to partition the classifier's output range [0, 1] into multiple segments and associate each with a distinct sub-filter. By aligning the decision structure with the classifier's confidence scores, the filter can respond more appropriately to varying levels of uncertainty in predictions.

A g-SLBF consists of a learned model f, and a set of g stable Bloom filters $\text{SBF}_1, \ldots, \text{SBF}_g$, each tailored to handle a specific subrange of prediction scores. Formally, the interval [0, 1] is divided into g subintervals: $[\tau_0 = 0, \tau_1], [\tau_1, \tau_2], \ldots, [\tau_{g-1}, \tau_g = 1]$, and a query element x is directed to the corresponding SBF_j based on the score $f(x)$. Each sub-filter is independently parameterized as $(m_j, K_j, P_j, \text{Max}_j)$, offering finer control over storage and false positive behavior across different confidence levels. The architecture is illustrated in Fig. 4.2.

Notably, s-SLBF can be interpreted as a specific instance of g-SLBF when $g = 2$, in which one sub-filter unconditionally accommodates all elements classified as positive based on a single threshold τ. In contrast, a g-SLBF with $g > 2$ avoids overcommitting to the classifier's decisions. By jointly relying on both the model and the backup filters for all score intervals, g-SLBF achieves greater robustness, especially in situations where the classifier encounters inputs outside its training distribution or when prediction confidence is unreliable.

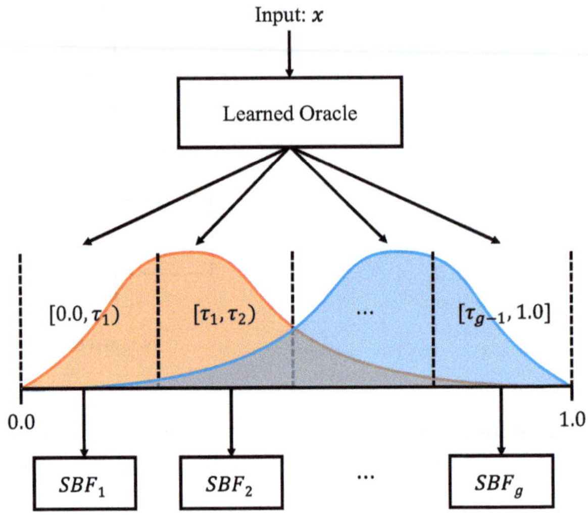

Fig. 4.2 Illustration of g-SLBF

4.2.2 Operations: Insertion and Query Mechanisms

SLBF primarily supports two key procedures: **insert**, for incorporating a new element x into the filter, and **query**, for determining whether a given input y should be treated as part of the set.

4.2.2.1 Single SLBF

The insertion of an element x (Algorithm 15) begins by feeding x into the predictive model f to obtain a confidence score. This score is then compared to a specified threshold τ. If $f(x) \geq \tau$, the system assumes x is already represented implicitly and skips further processing. If the confidence falls short, the element is explicitly stored in the SBF backend.

To illustrate the insertion process in s-SLBF, consider a scenario where the threshold is set to $\tau = 0.85$. The SBF is configured with parameters $(m = 1000, K = 4, P = 3, \text{Max} = 5)$, allowing it to handle continuous insertions while limiting false negatives.

Suppose we are processing a stream of URLs for membership testing. An incoming URL x_1 is evaluated by the model, which returns a score of $f(x_1) = 0.92$. Since this exceeds τ, the system assumes the URL is already represented in the learned model and skips inserting it into the SBF.

Next, another URL x_2 arrives with $f(x_2) = 0.76$. As this falls below the threshold, it is explicitly inserted into the SBF.

Algorithm 15 s-SLBF: Insertion

```
Input: A structure (f, τ, SBF) and a stream x_1, ..., x_N
for i = 1 to N do
    if f(x_i) ≥ τ then
        continue
    else
        Insert x_i into SBF
    end if
end for
```

Algorithm 16 s-SLBF: Query

```
Input: SLBF instance (f, τ, SBF) and query y
score ← f(y)
if score ≥ τ then
    return true
else
    return result from SBF
end if
```

To process a query for y (Algorithm 16), the confidence score $f(y)$ is used to drive the response. If the score exceeds the threshold, the query returns a positive result immediately. Otherwise, the result is delegated to the SBF layer for final judgment.

To demonstrate the query mechanism in s-SLBF, suppose the filter uses a threshold $\tau = 0.85$, and the SBF is configured with parameters ($m = 1000$, $K = 4$, $P = 3$, Max $= 5$). The model f assigns confidence scores between 0 and 1 to each query.

Consider a query for an element y_1 where the model returns $f(y_1) = 0.88$. Since this score exceeds the threshold τ, the system immediately returns `true`, without consulting the SBF.

Now consider another query for element y_2, where $f(y_2) = 0.72$. As this falls below τ, the system forwards the query to the SBF for evaluation. If the SBF reports `false`, then the final result is `false`.

4.2.2.2 Grouping SLBF

As demonstrated in Fig. 4.2, the grouped SLBF (g-SLBF) leverages a partitioned strategy by dividing the confidence spectrum into multiple bins, each associated with a dedicated sub-filter. This design allows the filter to fine-tune its false positive and negative trade-offs based on classifier performance across confidence levels.

Elements exhibiting low confidence scores (typically on the left side of the distribution) are more susceptible to classifier mistakes, especially false positives. To mitigate this, their respective sub-filters SBF_j are aggressively configured using tighter parameter sets like K, P, and Max to reduce error rates. Fewer elements fall into this region due to high recall, meaning fewer counters are necessary.

Algorithm 17 g-SLBF: Insertion

Input: Model f, sub-filters $SBF_1, \ldots, SBF_g$, and elements $x_1, \ldots, x_N$
for $i = 1$ to N **do**
  Identify index j such that $f(x_i) \in [\tau_{j-1}, \tau_j]$
  Insert x_i into SBF_j
end for

Algorithm 18 g-SLBF: Query

Input: Model f, sub-filters $SBF_1, \ldots, SBF_g$, and query y
Identify index j such that $f(y) \in [\tau_{j-1}, \tau_j]$
return result from SBF_j

On the other end, elements with high classifier confidence (on the right of the distribution) are likely genuine members. Here, the sub-filters can relax their false positive constraints. However, as the classifier may miss some true positives in this range, these filters must be provisioned with more counters to maintain convergence and accuracy.

For insertion (Algorithm 17), each incoming x is routed to the appropriate SBF_j based on which confidence bucket its score belongs to.

To demonstrate the insertion mechanism in g-SLBF, suppose the classifier's output range [0, 1] is divided into three intervals:

$$[\tau_0 = 0, \tau_1 = 0.4], \quad [\tau_1 = 0.4, \tau_2 = 0.7], \quad [\tau_2 = 0.7, \tau_3 = 1],$$

with each interval associated with a dedicated sub-filter:

– SBF_1: ($m = 500, K = 3, P = 2, \text{Max} = 3$)—for low-confidence predictions
– SBF_2: ($m = 700, K = 4, P = 2, \text{Max} = 5$)—for medium-confidence predictions
– SBF_3: ($m = 800, K = 5, P = 1, \text{Max} = 10$)—for high-confidence predictions

Now consider a stream of elements being inserted. An element x_1 arrives with a model score $f(x_1) = 0.25$, placing it in the first interval [0, 0.4]. The system routes this element to SBF_1 and inserts it there.

Next, an element x_2 with $f(x_2) = 0.68$ falls into the second interval [0.4, 0.7], so it is inserted into SBF_2.

Finally, an element x_3 with $f(x_3) = 0.85$ belongs to the third interval [0.7, 1] and is therefore stored in SBF_3.

For a query (Algorithm 18), the same mapping applies: the classifier score determines which sub-filter should handle the lookup.

To illustrate the query process in g-SLBF, consider the same configuration where the classifier's output space is partitioned into three intervals:

$$[\tau_0 = 0, \tau_1 = 0.4], \quad [\tau_1 = 0.4, \tau_2 = 0.7], \quad [\tau_2 = 0.7, \tau_3 = 1],$$

with corresponding sub-filters SBF_1, SBF_2, and SBF_3.

Suppose a query is made for an element y_1 with $f(y_1) = 0.33$. Since this score lies in the first interval [0, 0.4], the system routes the query to SBF_1. If SBF_1 reports `false`, then the overall result is `false`.

In another case, a query is issued for element y_2 with $f(y_2) = 0.75$, which falls into the third interval [0.7, 1]. The query is forwarded to SBF_3. If SBF_3 returns `true`, the final result is `true`.

4.2.3 Analysis: Error Rates and Time Complexity

A theoretical analysis is conducted on the FPR, FNR, and time complexity of the proposed s-SLBF and g-SLBF. The analysis primarily centers on g-SLBF, as s-SLBF can be regarded as a specific configuration of g-SLBF with only one sub-filter. Consequently, all theoretical guarantees derived for g-SLBF directly apply to s-SLBF.

4.2.3.1 False Positive Rate

When the classifier outputs a score falling into the j-th range $[\tau_{j-1}, \tau_j]$, let p_j denote the probability that a non-member falls into this range. The expected FPR of g-SLBF at the stable state is

$$\mathbf{E}[FPR] = \sum_{j=1}^{g} p_j \cdot \alpha_j, \quad \text{where } \alpha_j = \left(1 - \left(\frac{1}{1 + \frac{K_j}{P_j}}\right)^{\text{Max}_j}\right)^{K_j}. \tag{4.9}$$

An upper bound of the expected FPR can be given by the average of all sub-filter FPRs:

$$\mathbf{E}[FPR] \leq \frac{1}{g} \sum_{j=1}^{g} \alpha_j. \tag{4.10}$$

4.2.3.2 False Negative Rate

FN occurs when previously inserted elements are removed due to limited counter capacity. Assuming each element is inserted only once and queried after a gap δ, the expected FNR is

$$\mathbf{E}[FNR] = \sum_{j=1}^{g} q_j \cdot \beta_j, \quad \text{where } \beta_j = \left(1 - \left(1 - p_N(\delta, K_j)\right)^{K_j}\right). \tag{4.11}$$

where q_j is the probability a member falls in the j-th range and $p_N(\delta, K_j)$ is the probability that a counter associated with the element is decremented to zero after δ insertions.

4.2.3.3 Time Complexity

Assuming model inference takes $O(M)$ time, the overall insertion and query complexities are

$$O\left(M + \max_j(P_j + K_j)\right) \quad \text{and} \quad O\left(M + \max_j K_j\right), \tag{4.12}$$

which are constant in practice since M, P_j, and K_j are fixed.

4.3 Learned Cuckoo Filter (LCF)

Stable Bloom filters and their learned extensions (e.g., Stable Learned Bloom filter) represent early attempts to strike a balance between accuracy and space in streaming membership queries. These designs typically rely on fixed-size sliding windows and probabilistic decay mechanisms, which work well under constrained scenarios but fall short when query granularity varies or precision demands shift.

Learned Cuckoo filter (LCF) [4] introduces a hybrid approach that decouples memory layout from fixed-time semantics. By combining a chain of Cuckoo filters [5] with a frequency-aware prediction model, LCF selectively retains relevant data and adapts its response to a wide range of query window sizes.

4.3.1 Structure: Baseline and Compact Designs

LCF integrates two key components to handle approximate membership queries over data streams: a sequence of Cuckoo filters and a prediction model that guides long-range estimations. Depending on the trade-off between simplicity and space efficiency, two instantiations of this design are introduced—a baseline form (LCF-B) and a compact variant (LCF-C)—each with distinct structural characteristics.

4.3.1.1 LCF-B

LCF-B maintains a rolling buffer of fixed-capacity Cuckoo filters, where each filter stores the fingerprints of recently seen elements. As new data arrives, elements are appended to the newest filter until it reaches its predefined capacity. At that point,

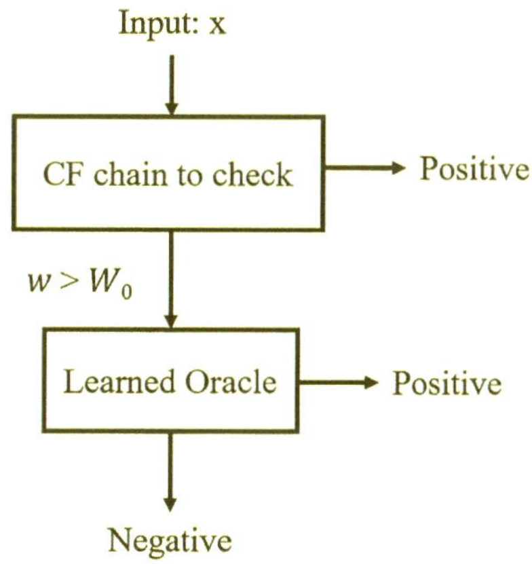

Fig. 4.3 Illustration of LCF

a fresh filter is allocated, and if the memory budget is exceeded, the oldest one is evicted. This creates a bounded, sliding archive of recent activity. To compensate for data beyond this range, LCF-B augments the filter chain with a learned model trained to estimate the recurrence interval of elements. This model—referred to as an oracle—serves as a fallback to support longer queries: if the filters cannot confirm presence, the oracle's prediction is used to infer membership.

Structurally, LCF-B is modular and straightforward in design. Each filter in the sequence operates independently and maintains no knowledge of the rest. The oracle is queried only when the specified window size exceeds the default range covered by the current filter chain. The architecture is illustrated in Fig. 4.3.

4.3.1.2 LCF-C

LCF-C extends the baseline design by aggressively trimming redundancy to reduce space overhead. Instead of allowing multiple copies of the same fingerprint to exist across filters, LCF-C actively removes outdated versions of elements as new ones arrive. This is done with guidance from the same oracle used for querying: by estimating the likely position of an earlier occurrence, the system targets and removes previous entries during updates.

To further economize on space, LCF-C introduces a reorganization mechanism that periodically compacts sparse filters. Filters with excessive empty slots are partially merged by redistributing their valid entries into a smaller footprint, allowing redundant space to be reclaimed. This structural optimization helps maintain high load factors and sustains insertion performance even under limited memory budgets.

4.3.2 Operation: Insertion, Query, and Update Mechanisms

This section describes how the Learned Cuckoo filter operates in practice, covering both the baseline (LCF-B) and the compact (LCF-C) variants. We outline their respective procedures for insertion, query, and update and provide detailed examples to illustrate the underlying logic. Each operation is followed by a formal pseudocode representation.

4.3.2.1 Insertion Mechanism in LCF-B

The baseline variant, LCF-B, manages recent stream elements through a chain of Cuckoo filters. Each filter can hold up to κ elements. New elements are inserted into the most recent filter $\mathcal{F}[1]$; when it fills up, a new filter is prepended to the chain. This rolling structure helps retain only the freshest data while preventing duplication of fingerprints across filters. The insertion counter c tracks the number of elements inserted into the current filter and resets whenever a new filter is created.

To illustrate the process, consider a case where $\mathcal{F}[1]$ holds fingerprints for elements $\{7, 2\}$ and the counter is $c = 2$. A new element $e = 9$ arrives. Since the current filter is not full and nine is not already present, it is inserted, and c is incremented to 3. Then, if another element $e = 5$ arrives, the filter is now full, triggering the creation of a new empty filter. This new filter becomes the new $\mathcal{F}[1]$, and five is inserted into it with the counter reset. The formal insertion logic is shown in Algorithm 19.

4.3.2.2 Query Mechanism in LCF-B

To determine if a queried element q was seen within a sliding window of size w, LCF-B scans a subset of the filter chain. Specifically, it checks the most recent $s = \lceil w/\kappa \rceil$ filters for a matching fingerprint. Suppose the element is not found and the requested window exceeds a predefined default window W_0. In that case,

---

Algorithm 19 LCF-B: Insertion

Input: New element e
Data: Filter list $\mathcal{F}$, insertion counter c
if $c < \kappa$ **and** e not in $\mathcal{F}[1]$ **then**
  Insert fingerprint of e into $\mathcal{F}[1]$
else
  Create a new empty filter and prepend to $\mathcal{F}$
  Insert e into the new head filter $\mathcal{F}[1]$
  Reset $c \leftarrow 0$
end if
Increment $c \leftarrow c + 1$

Algorithm 20 LCF-B: Membership query

Input: Query element q, window size $window\_size$
Data: Filter list $\mathcal{F}$, oracle $\mathcal{M}$, threshold W_0
// Determine number of filters to check based on window size
$num\_filters \leftarrow \min\left(|\mathcal{F}|, \lceil \frac{window\_size}{\kappa} \rceil\right)$
for $i = 1$ to $num\_filters$ **do**
    if q is contained in $\mathcal{F}[i]$ **then**
        return `True`
    end if
end for
// Early rejection for small windows
if $window\_size \leq W_0$ **then**
    return `False`
end if
Estimate gap prediction $\hat{g}_q \leftarrow \mathcal{M}(q)$
// Check if predicted gap falls within current window range
if $W_0 < \hat{g}_q \leq window\_size$ **then**
    return `True`
else
    return `False`
end if

the system invokes a learned model to estimate whether the element might still be considered "recent" based on its expected reoccurrence pattern.

For example, suppose $\kappa = 3$, $w = 5$, and $W_0 = 4$. The filter chain includes $\mathcal{F}[1]$ with $\{9, 5\}$ and $\mathcal{F}[2]$ with $\{7, 2, 8\}$. If we query for 7, it is found in $\mathcal{F}[2]$, and the result is `True`. If we instead query for 6, which appears nowhere, and ask for a window $w = 5 > W_0$, the model estimates $\hat{g}_6 = 6$. Since this is not within the query range, the result is `False`. The detailed query procedure is outlined in Algorithm 20.

4.3.2.3 Update Mechanism in LCF-C

The compact variant LCF-C improves memory efficiency by removing outdated copies of repeating elements. When a new occurrence of an element arrives, LCF-C predicts where previous instances might have been stored and deletes them before inserting the new one. This process uses the same learned model to estimate recurrence intervals and focuses the deletion within a bounded region defined by tunable offsets γ_1 and γ_2. If no prior copy is found, the operation proceeds like LCF-B.

Consider an example with $\kappa = 3$, $c = 1$, and a filter chain consisting of $\mathcal{F}[1]$ with $\{9\}$, $\mathcal{F}[2]$ with $\{3, 7\}$, and $\mathcal{F}[3]$ with $\{5\}$. When element 7 arrives again, the model predicts a gap $\hat{g}_7 = 4$. Using this and the current counter $c = 1$, we compute the target search range to be only $\mathcal{F}[2]$. There, the older copy of 7 is found and removed. The new fingerprint is then inserted into $\mathcal{F}[1]$. The complete update logic is shown in Algorithm 21.

Algorithm 21 LCF-C: Update

Input: Element e
Data: Filter list $\mathcal{F}$, oracle model $\mathcal{M}$, counter c
Parameters: Search bounds γ_1, γ_2
if $c < \kappa$ **and** e not in $\mathcal{F}[1]$ **then**
  Predict recurrence gap: $\hat{g}_e \leftarrow \mathcal{M}(e)$
  Compute:
    $i_{\text{start}} \leftarrow \left\lceil \frac{\hat{g}_e - c}{\kappa} \right\rceil + \gamma_1$
    $i_{\text{end}} \leftarrow \left\lceil \frac{\hat{g}_e - c}{\kappa} \right\rceil - \gamma_2$
  for $i = i_{\text{start}}$ to i_{end} **do**
    Remove fingerprint of e from $\mathcal{F}[i]$ if present
  end for
  Insert fingerprint of e into $\mathcal{F}[1]$
else
  Follow LCF-B insertion procedure (Algorithm 19)
end if
Increment counter $c \leftarrow c + 1$

4.3.3 *Analysis: Error Rates and Time Complexity*

We present a theoretical analysis of the LCF, focusing on its FPR, FNR, and time complexity. These results characterize the accuracy and efficiency of LCF when deployed in dynamic data stream environments.

4.3.3.1 False Positive Rate

FPs in LCF may arise either from the fingerprint collisions within the Cuckoo filter chain or from misclassifications by the learned model when the filters fail to match.

Assuming a query over a window of size w, let κ denote the capacity of each individual Cuckoo filter. Then the number of filters scanned is $s = \lceil w/\kappa \rceil$. Let f be the false positive probability of a single filter and $\text{FPR}_{\mathcal{M}}(w)$ the probability that the model incorrectly predicts presence within window w. The overall expected FPR is given by

$$\mathbf{E}[\text{FPR}(w)] = 1 - (1 - f)^s + (1 - f)^s \cdot \text{FPR}_{\mathcal{M}}(w). \tag{4.13}$$

The first term accounts for collisions within the filters, while the second reflects the contribution from model-level mispredictions when filters return negative.

4.3.3.2 False Negative Rate

FNs occur when a queried element has already been evicted from all active filters, and the model also fails to predict its presence.

Let $\mathrm{FNR}_{\mathcal{M}}(w)$ denote the false negative probability of the model on a window of size w, and let $P_{\mathrm{evict}}(w)$ be the probability that the element has aged beyond the s most recent filters. Then the expected FNR is

$$\mathbf{E}[\mathrm{FNR}(w)] = P_{\mathrm{evict}}(w) \cdot \mathrm{FNR}_{\mathcal{M}}(w). \tag{4.14}$$

Here, $P_{\mathrm{evict}}(w) = \mathbb{P}[\mathrm{age}(e) > s \cdot \kappa]$, which depends on the data arrival distribution and filter maintenance policy.

4.3.3.3 Time Complexity

A membership query involves scanning at most $s = \lceil w/\kappa \rceil$ filters in sequence, followed optionally by a model inference step. If model evaluation takes $O(M)$ time, the total query complexity is

$$T_{\mathrm{query}}(w) = O\left(\left\lceil \frac{w}{\kappa} \right\rceil + M\right). \tag{4.15}$$

In typical settings, both κ and M are constant or small, making the query cost effectively constant with respect to stream size.

4.4 Summary and Comparison

The field of streaming filters has evolved significantly to meet the demands of approximate membership queries over continuous, high-velocity data streams. Unlike traditional static filters such as Bloom filters, streaming filters are designed to dynamically manage element lifetimes while maintaining bounded memory usage and controllable error rates.

This chapter introduced three representative streaming filters: SBF [1], SLBF [3], and LCF [4]. Each offers a unique approach to balancing accuracy, efficiency, and adaptability in dynamic environments.

4.4.1 Summary of Streaming Filters

- **Stable Bloom filter**. SBF builds upon the classical BF by replacing bits with multi-bit counters that support gradual decay. This enables SBF to maintain a stable false positive rate even under continuous insertions, making it suitable for scenarios where memory is limited and model-free operation is preferred.
- **Stable Learned Bloom filter**. SLBF integrates learned models into the filtering process, enhancing space efficiency by delegating confidence decisions to a

Table 4.1 Comparison of streaming filters

Feature/method	SBF	SLBF (g-SLBF)	LCF (LCF-C)
Structure	Multi-bit counter array	Model + group of SBFs	Chain of Cuckoo filters + oracle
Error types	FP + FN	FP + FN	FP + FN
Time complexity	$O(1)$	$O(M + K)$	$O(\lceil w/\kappa \rceil + M)$
Model dependency	No	Yes	Yes
Adaptability	Fixed window only	Adjustable via thresholds	Variable window support
Space efficiency	Moderate	High	Very high
Main advantage	Stability, simplicity	Learning-enhanced efficiency	Flexible querying, compaction
Key limitation	Less adaptive	Model sensitivity	Higher implementation complexity
Typical use case	General-purpose stream filtering	Resource-constrained classification	Dynamic query workloads

classifier. SLBF comes in two forms: single SLBF and grouped SLBF, with the latter offering better robustness by partitioning prediction scores into multiple sub-filters.

- **Learned Cuckoo filter**. LCF combines cuckoo hashing with frequency-aware prediction models to offer variable window querying. It features a baseline variant (LCF-B) for simplicity and a compact variant (LCF-C) for improved space utilization through proactive eviction and compaction.

4.4.2 Comparison of Streaming Filters

To provide a comprehensive view of their characteristics, Table 4.1 compares these methods across key dimensions: structural design, error types, time complexity, advantages, limitations, and typical use cases.

4.4.3 Conclusion

Each of the discussed filters represents a significant advancement in the domain of streaming data management. SBF provides a robust, model-free solution ideal for general-purpose applications. SLBF introduces learning to reduce space overhead, but at the cost of increased dependency on model quality. LCF further refines this concept by enabling flexible window sizes and efficient space reclamation, making it well-suited for real-world systems with unpredictable query patterns.

Choosing among these filters depends on specific application requirements, including available memory, tolerance to errors, computational resources, and the need for adaptability. Understanding their trade-offs allows practitioners to make informed decisions when designing scalable and accurate stream processing systems.

References

1. Deng, F., Rafiei, D.: Approximately detecting duplicates for streaming data using stable bloom filters. In: Proceedings of ACM SIGMOD International Conference on Management of Data, pp. 25–36 (2006). https://doi.org/10.1145/1142473.1142477
2. Bloom, B.H.: Space/time trade-offs in hash coding with allowable errors. Commun. ACM 422–426 (1970). https://doi.org/10.1145/362686.362692
3. Liu, Q., Zheng, L., Shen, Y., et al.: Stable learned bloom filters for data streams. Proc. VLDB Endow. 2355–2367 (2020). https://doi.org/10.14778/3407790.3407830
4. Tian, Y., Yan, T., Zhang, R., et al.: A learned cuckoo filter for approximate membership queries over variable-sized sliding windows on data streams. Proc. ACM Manag. Data **264**(27), 1–264 (2023). https://doi.org/10.1145/3626758
5. Fan, B., Andersen, D.G., Kaminsky M., et al.: Cuckoo filter: Practically better than bloom. In: Proceedings of the 10th ACM International on Conference on emerging Networking Experiments and Technologies, pp. 75–88 (2014). https://doi.org/10.1145/2674005.2674994
6. Kraska, T., Beutel, A., Chi, E.H., et al.: The case for learned index structures. In: Proceedings of ACM SIGMOD International Conference on Management of Data, pp. 489–504 (2018). https://doi.org/10.1145/3183713.3196909

References

Choosing among these filters depends on specific application requirements, including [illegible] tolerance to errors, computational resources, and the need for [illegible]. Understanding their trade-offs allows practitioners to make informed decisions when designing scalable and robust [illegible] processing systems.

References

[illegible]

Chapter 5
Range Filters

Abstract Range filters aim to efficiently determine the existence of elements within a specified range. They guarantee query results without false negatives. Due to such reliability, they are widely used in practical scenarios to avoid accessing empty ranges. Numerous studies have consistently demonstrated that range filters can significantly enhance the overall range query performance by preemptively filtering out empty ranges, thereby reducing I/O operations and computational overhead. This chapter introduces six representative range filters, detailing their implementation specifics and analyzing their theoretical performance.

Keywords Range query · Range filters

Range filters constitute a specialized class of probabilistic data structures, aiming to efficiently execute range queries while preserving the accuracy of point queries. These filters achieve low time complexity by leveraging compact in-memory representations, making them particularly suitable for LSM-tree-based storage systems where space efficiency is crucial. Characterized by their one-sided error property (allowing false positives but not false negatives), range filters optimize query performance by eliminating unnecessary disk accesses. When a key is determined to be absent during the initial in-memory filter check, the system can avoid loading the corresponding SSTable altogether.

The architectural landscape of range filters encompasses four fundamental designs. This chapter systematically examines each architectural approach, analyzing their respective design principles and performance trade-offs. Prefix-based variants like ARF and SuRF employ tree structures such as binary tries to facilitate large-range queries; hash-based implementations including Rosetta and BloomRF utilize layered Bloom filters or monotonic hash functions to handle smaller ranges while improving robustness through suffix-aware hashing; learned approaches exemplified by SNARF adopt linear regression models to approximate data distributions, offering particularly efficient performance for non-correlated query patterns; and hybrid designs such as Proteus combine multiple techniques to capitalize on their complementary strengths.

H. Dai et al., *Advanced Filter Structure Handbook*,
https://doi.org/10.1007/978-981-95-1715-2_5

The selection of an appropriate filter type, guided by specific data distribution characteristics and query workload patterns, can yield substantial improvements in overall system efficiency.

5.1 Adaptive Range Filter (ARF)

Adaptive Range Filter (ARF) [1] is an innovative indexing structure designed to address range filtering challenges within Microsoft Research's Project Siberia. This project explores thermal data management methodologies for Hekaton, an in-memory database engine optimized for high throughput. The framework autonomously relocates cold data to cost-efficient secondary storage while retaining hot data in primary memory, thereby accelerating queries targeting exclusively hot data segments.

ARF is a trie-based indexing structure optimized for range query processing. Functionally, it operates as a specialized variant of the Bloom filter, adapted specifically for range-based membership testing. ARF supports indexing over arbitrary ordered domains and enables efficient probabilistic verification of range query matches. Like standard Bloom filters, ARF maintains key advantages in query latency, space efficiency, and graceful performance degradation under increasing false positive ratio (FPR).

A defining characteristic of ARFs lies in their adaptive capability. The structure continuously self-optimizes by analyzing query patterns and underlying data distributions. Initialized in an empty state, ARFs progressively refine their configuration through query processing, incorporating feedback mechanisms (e.g., FPR) to guide adjustments. This adaptation manifests through precise indexing of high-value domain regions while maintaining coarse representations for less frequented areas. Notably, ARFs maintain this dynamic adaptability when confronted with workload variations or data distribution shifts.

5.1.1 Structure: Binary Tree

ARF is fundamentally implemented as a binary tree, with leaf nodes representing discrete key ranges and encoding the presence of records in cold storage. Each leaf node contains an occupied bit that denotes whether its associated range includes any valid records. For example, the ARF depicted in Fig. 2.1 signals potential records in ranges [0, 7] and [12, 12], as their occupied bits are set to true. Conversely, it definitively excludes records in ranges [8, 11], [13, 13], and [14, 15], as their corresponding bits are false.

Non-leaf nodes in an ARF serve as navigational anchors during query processing, directing traversal toward leaves that satisfy the query constraints. Each intermediate node partitions its assigned key range into two equal subranges, delegating the left and right halves to its respective child nodes. The root node, as the apex of this hierarchy, spans the complete domain of the indexed attribute. This binary subdivision enables logarithmic-time search by systematically narrowing the query space at each level.

The ARF structure achieves inherent space efficiency through its implicit range representation. By recursively partitioning domains into equal halves at each node, the design eliminates the need for explicit range-boundary storage. This implicit addressing mechanism yields a compact encoding, where node ranges are derived computationally rather than stored physically. As a trie-based structure, each ARF level corresponds to a progressively significant bit in the domain's binary representation. Consequently, the complete ARF encoding requires only the domain's logical boundaries, the trie's topological structure, and the occupancy status bits at leaf nodes. This triple encoding ensures minimal storage overhead while maintaining full query functionality.

To illustrate concretely, each intermediate node can be denoted with two bits encoding the presence of 0, 1, or 2 children for the node:

- 00: Both children are leaves (e.g., Node [12, 13] in Fig. 5.1).
- 01: Left child is a leaf; right child is an intermediate node (e.g., Node [8, 15] in Fig. 5.1).
- 10: Left child is an intermediate node; right child is a leaf (e.g., Node [12, 15] in Fig. 5.1).
- 11: Both children are intermediate nodes (e.g., Node [0, 15] in Fig. 5.1).

The shape of an entire ARF is encoded by serializing the intermediate nodes during a breadth-first traversal. Take the ARF shown in Fig. 5.1 as an example; it is encoded with the following bit sequence: 01 01 10 00.

In addition to the bit sequence encoding the intermediate nodes, an ARF also retains the status of occupied bits in the leaves. Continuing with the example of Fig. 5.1, the leaf bit sequence is 10100. When merging the shape encoding

Fig. 5.1 Example ARF

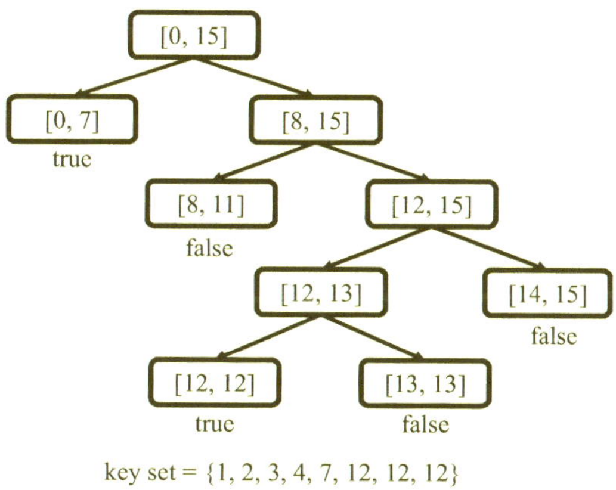

(intermediate node bits) and leaf occupied bits, the ARF in Fig. 5.1 is compressed into 13 bits.

Generally, an ARF with n nodes is encoded using approximately $1.5n$ bits, structured as:

- $2 \times \frac{n}{2}$ bits for intermediate nodes
- $\frac{n}{2} + 1$ bits for leaves

This formula aligns with the example: for n $= 8$, 8 bits (intermediate) + 5 bits (leaves) $= 13$ bits total.

5.1.2 Operation: Query, Escalation, and De-escalation

To process a range query [l, r], the ARF initiates a top-down traversal from the root node to the leaf corresponding to the lower bound l. A positive occupied bit at this leaf triggers an immediate positive filter response. Conversely, if the bit is unset (false), the algorithm iteratively examines the leaf's right sibling nodes until either a node with an active occupied bit is encountered (yielding a positive result), or the traversal reaches the leaf containing the upper bound r (confirming the range's absence in cold storage).

An appealing attribute of the ARF structure lies in its adaptability to both data and query distribution. We will explore methods for constructing and evolving an ARF to better accommodate changes in query patterns and data movement.

The escalation of an ARF, much like other tree-based structures, involves growth and reduction processes. It expands by splitting leaves and contracts through leaf merging. To illustrate this, Fig. 5.2 demonstrates the possible evolution of the ARF depicted in Fig. 5.1.

An ARF starts with a single node that represents the entire range. For the example in Figs. 5.1 and 5.2a shows this basic, initial ARF. Then, as shown in Fig. 5.2b, the ARF evolves when node [0, 15] is split. Further, Fig. 5.2c depicts the outcome of splitting node [8, 15], continuing the growth process of the ARF.

A distinctive feature of ARFs is their dynamic adaptation mechanism. Unlike conventional tree structures that modify their topology solely in response to data updates, ARFs autonomously adjust their structure based on observed query patterns and data distributions. This behavioral adaptation is formalized in Algorithm 22 through the escalation protocol. The fundamental premise is to trigger structural escalation when a range query q produces a false positive, thereby rectifying the error and preventing its recurrence in future queries.

The ARF does this by navigating to the leaf node containing q's left boundary q.left, repeatedly splitting this node until introducing a new leaf whose left boundary is exactly q.left, doing the symmetric operation for the right boundary q.right, and calling the MarkEmpty procedure to mark the occupied bits of all leaves between q.left and q.right as false, indicating this range truly contains no records in the cold store.

Fig. 5.2 Escalating an ARF. (**a**) Before escalation. (**b**) Firstly split. (**c**) Complect escalation

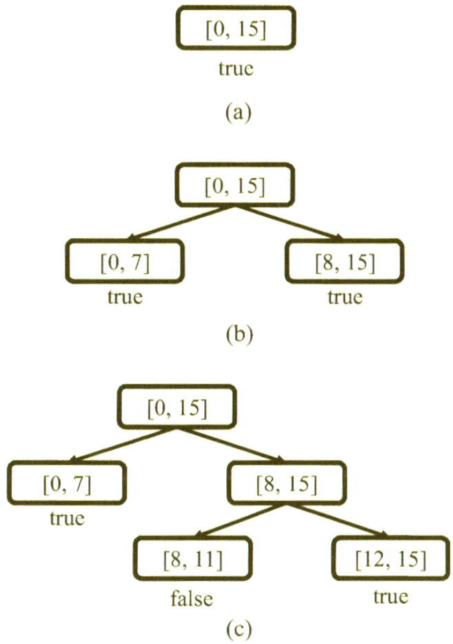

Algorithm 22 ARF escalation

```
function PROCESS(Query q)
...
    if q reports a false positive then
        node ← NAVIGATE (q.left)
        while (node.left ≠ q.left) & node.occupied do
            Split(node)
            node ← NAVIGATE (q.left)
        end while
        node ← NAVIGATE (q.right)
        while (node.right ≠ q.right) & node.occupied do
            Split(node)
            node ← NAVIGATE (q.right)
        end while
        MARKEMPTY(q.left, q.right)
    end if
...
end function
```

As a result of these splits, the ARF expands in size. When space constraints arise, the ARF undergoes de-escalation, a process that trades precision for spatial efficiency.

While escalation improves ARF's precision, de-escalation inherently reduces it by merging nodes. The critical challenge lies in identifying optimal merge candidate nodes with minimal probability of intersecting future queries, to avoid post-de-escalation false positives. To determine these nodes, the ARF employs a replacement policy. Space efficiency is crucial for ARFs, making this policy ideal.

Fig. 5.3 ARF de-escalation. (**a**) Before. (**b**) After

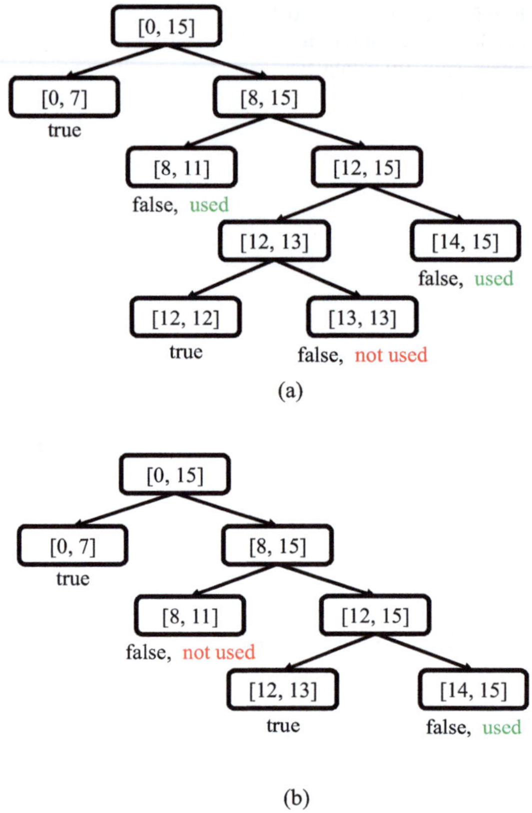

Figure 5.3 illustrates de-escalation using a clock policy, continuing the example from Fig. 5.1. In Fig. 5.3a, every leaf has a "used bit," which will be set if the query hits the corresponding leaf. As an example, handling query [9, 10] involves setting the used bit of leaf [8, 11]. This action signifies the leaf's relevance and renders it unsuitable for replacement. Moreover, the clock pointer indicates leaf [8, 11]. If the ARF exceeds its space limit, the replacement policy triggers: upon checking [8, 11], the policy finds its used bit set, moves the pointer to the next leaf, and unsets [8, 11]'s used bit. In this scenario, the clock policy designates leaf [13, 13] as the victim due to its unset used bit.

As shown in Fig. 5.3b, the ARF status following the de-escalation operation that replaces the [13, 13] entry is illustrated. This de-escalation mechanism functions by merging the victim node with its sibling node—here, the [12, 12] node specifically. De-escalation can only be executed when the sibling node is also a leaf node. In cases where this condition is unmet, the clock strategy continues to search for victim nodes until two leaf nodes are identified. Additionally, merge operations may cascade if the occupied bit values of the two leaf nodes are identical. For example, in the scenario depicted in Fig. 5.3b, the occupied bit values of Nodes [12, 13] and

Algorithm 23 ARF De-escalation

```
function PROCESS(Query q)
... //implement Escalation
    while size > budget do
        node1 ← FINDVICTIM
        node2 ← SIBLING(node1)
        MERGE(node1, node2)
    end while
end function
```

[14, 15] differ, thus halting the cascade of merge operations. It should be emphasized that used bits are only required for leaf nodes with their occupied bits set to false. These specific leaf nodes contain relevant information and need protection against replacement, which results in a 50% reduction in the space required to store usage statistics.

Algorithm 23 presents the pseudo-code for the full de-escalation procedure. This code executes immediately following any potential escalation operations. The *FindVictim* function implicitly manages clock progression and the resetting of used bits. The Sibling function determines the sibling node for a given leaf, and the Merge function initiates a cascade process when the occupied bit values of two sibling nodes are identical.

Escalation illustrates how an ARF adapts to false positive queries. In addition, there are two other methods to expedite the learning process of the ARF.

The first method is learning from true positives: when a query prompts access to the cold data, and it indeed returns a non-empty result, it is termed as a true positive. From these outcomes, the ARF can deduce additional vacant range information and update itself accordingly. For instance, if a query [5, 15] only returns two keys 7 and 9 it implies that the cold data lacks records within ranges [5, 6], [8, 8], and [10, 15]; thus, the occupied bit of the respective leaf node can be set.

The second method is proactively seeking supplementary information from the cold data: specifically, when accessing the cold data, querying intervals larger than the actual required range allows for subsequent filtration of unnecessary results. This approach of querying beyond the specified range can provide more vacant range information, expediting learning. For instance, when querying [13, 14], querying the complete interval of [12, 15] enables the exclusion of unnecessary expansions for the ARF if parts of this interval are empty.

To prevent false negative, when a record is relocated from the hot store to the cold store, all related ARF structures require an update. For example, in Fig. 5.1, when a record with key 10 is added to the cold store, the occupied bit of node [8, 11] must be set to true. This action ensures the range now includes a record, thereby preventing false negative outcomes. Notably, deleting a record from the cold store does not alter the ARF structure. Even if multiple records within node [11, 11] are known to have been removed, its occupied bit cannot be reset to false. Deletion only leads to inefficient false positives without causing correctness issues.

If permitted, an ARF can be initialized through a dedicated training phase, enabling it to perform optimally from the outset. The training algorithm involves the following steps:

- Explore Data: Scanning tables in the cold storage, constructing a precise ARF that accurately models all the gaps present in the cold storage. Essentially, this creates an unbounded escalated ARF.
- Explore Workloads: Running a series of representative example queries and updates to set the used bits (or usage counters) of leaf nodes. The aim is to learn the distribution of queries/updates.
- Meet Space Constraints: By employing Algorithm 23, appropriately trim the ARF to meet space constraints. Discard statistical information used for training, retaining only the runtime-used bits.

This training process results in an ARF that mirrors the workload and data distribution, precisely fitting hot spots within the allocated space. It minimizes unnecessary escalations and de-escalations from the outset. While adaptation can occur gradually without training through progressive optimization to adapt to queries, training expedites the convergence.

5.1.3 Analysis: FPR and Space

Regrettably, under constrained space budgets with fixed database and workload parameters, ARFs cannot guarantee minimal FPR due to the NP-hard nature of optimal range filter construction. Consequently, ARFs employ heuristic approximation to achieve practical performance.

Generally speaking, the probability of a false positive is on the same order as the average size of a leaf with its occupied bit set to true. As a result, the FPR has nothing to do with the query size.

It's not hard to demonstrate that finding an optimal ARF is an NP-hard problem for a Uniform workload and also in the general situation. We can prove this by making a reduction to the knapsack problem: the capacity of the knapsack corresponds to the space budget constraint of the filter. The weights of the items that need to be packed into the knapsack are equivalent to the size of the gaps between two different values in the cold store.

ARFs make an effort to get close to the solution of the knapsack problem. When a false positive takes place, ARFs gradually try to enhance the allocation of leaf nodes. In the absence of knowledge about the actual data and workload distributions, any real-world system has to depend on estimates and heuristics.

Buffer replacement policies and ARFs meet when dealing with a similar challenge: both methods strive to approximate the solution of the knapsack problem. This is accomplished by giving priority to keeping the objects in the cache that are most likely to be used soon. For example, ARFs can adopt a clock replacement policy to imitate the theoretically optimal algorithm. This offers a straightforward and efficient heuristic when no extra information is accessible.

5.2 Succinct Range Filter (SuRF)

Similar to ARF, the Succinct Range Filter (SuRF) [2] is an efficient, space-optimized data structure for range filtering. Unlike traditional Bloom filters, SuRF supports not only point queries but also various range queries, including open-range, closed-range, and range count operations. Built on the Fast Succinct Trie (FST), SuRF achieves point and range query performance on par with state-of-the-art order-preserving indexes while using just 10 bits per node. Additionally, it provides tunable FPR for both query types, making it adaptable to different application needs.

SuRF differs from ARF in terms of application focus and scalability objectives. An ARF instance performs optimally when handling specific query patterns it was trained for, but requires rebuilding—involving decoding, retraining, and re-encoding—if the query pattern shifts, which makes it function more like a cache than a general-purpose filter. By contrast, SuRF makes no assumptions about workload distributions, serving as a Bloom filter alternative with built-in range filtering capabilities. Additionally, ARF's binary tree architecture struggles with variable-length string keys, whereas SuRF natively supports such keys through its trie design. Finally, ARF employs linear scans across entire levels during tree traversal, a complexity that hinders scalability. SuRF avoids linear scans by leveraging efficient rank and select operations to navigate its internal tree structure.

5.2.1 Structure: Fast Succinct Trie (FST)

The core data structure of SuRF is the Fast Succinct Trie (FST), a compact static trie designed to efficiently process both point and range queries. This structure achieves performance comparable to or even superior to state-of-the-art pointer-based indexes. The FST design is rooted in the observation that the upper levels of a trie contain fewer nodes but undergo frequent accesses, whereas the lower levels consist of the majority of nodes but are accessed less frequently To address this, SuRF employs a fast bitmap-based encoding scheme (LOUDS-Dense) for upper trie levels, optimizing for performance by enabling child node searches with a single array lookup—prioritizing speed over strict space efficiency. For lower levels, SuRF uses the space-optimized LOUDS-Sparse scheme to ensure the encoded trie maintains a bounded overall size.

LOUDS-DS represents a hybrid trie architecture where upper levels utilize LOUDS-Dense encoding and lower levels adopt LOUDS-Sparse. The boundary between these levels is tunable, allowing trade-offs between performance and space consumption. The FST emphasizes maintaining a small number of upper levels

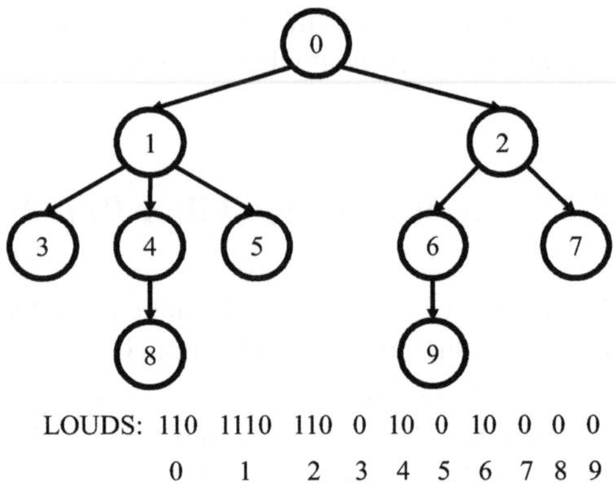

Fig. 5.4 Ordinal tree encoded with LOUDS

to leverage the space efficiency of LOUDS-Sparse. SuRF maintains a size ratio R between LOUDS-Sparse and LOUDS-Dense, which defines the hierarchical boundary for this optimization.

5.2.1.1 Level-Ordered Unary Degree Sequence

Jacobson pioneered research on succinct tree representations and developed the Level-Ordered Unary Degree Sequence (LOUDS) for encoding ordinal trees. As the name implies, LOUDS traverses nodes via breadth-first order and encodes each node's degree using unary code. For instance, Node 1 shown in Fig. 5.4 has three children, so it is encoded as 1110.

When navigating a tree encoded via LOUDS, the traversal process employs rank and select primitives. For a bit vector, $rank_1(i)$ computes the number of 1's up to position i (with $rank_0(i)$ counting the 0's), while $select_1(i)$ returns the position of the i-th 1 (and $select_0(i)$ locates the i-th 0).

To achieve constant-time complexity, rank and select operations leverage lookup tables (LUTs) storing precalculated outcomes, forming a sampling-based strategy. This approach minimizes the need to traverse the entire sequence by providing sampled data points, thus optimizing the traversal efficiency for LOUDS-encoded tree structures. Assume that node/child indices and bit positions start from zero, leading to the following properties.

- The position of the i-th node is given by $select_0(i) + 1$.
- The position of a k-th child of a node starting at position p is given by $select_0(rank_1(p + k)) + 1$.
- The position of the parent node for a node starting at p is given by $select_1(rank_0(p))$.

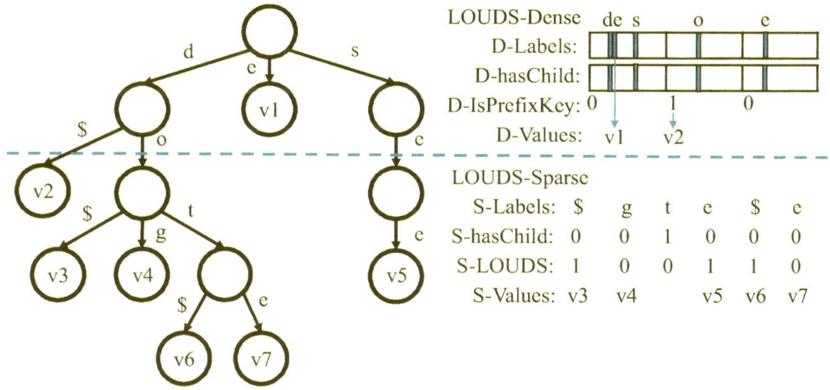

Fig. 5.5 Example trie encoded with LOUDS-DS

5.2.1.2 LOUDS-Dense

LOUDS-Dense sacrifices encoding efficiency in favor of improved query performance. To encode each node, LOUDS-Dense utilizes three 256-bitmaps, along with a byte sequence, to store values associated with each key. The encoding follows level order:

- D-Labels: Record of branch labels for each node. More precisely, the i-th bit within the bitmap indicates whether a branch with label i is present for the node.
- D-HasChild: Record signifying whether each branch has child nodes.
- D-IsPrefixKey: Recording whether the prefix itself is a key.
- D-Values: Storing fixed-length values associated with each key, for instance, the pointers.

Take the root node in Fig. 5.5 as an example: it has three branches labeled **d**, **e**, and **s**. Accordingly, the D-Labels bitmap sets the 100th, 101st, and 115th bits. While the **d** and **s** branches extend into sub-tries, the **e** branch terminates with a value. Under this scenario, only the 100th and 115th bits of the D-HasChild bitmap are set for the node. Furthermore, since **d** serves not only as a prefix but also as an actual key, the corresponding bit in the D-IsPrefixKey bitmap must be activated.

We denote $rank_1/select_1$ over bit sequence bs on position pos to be $rank_1$ / $select_1(bs, pos)$. Tree navigation on LOUDS-Dense is as follows:

- **Move Down**: For a given position pos where D-HasChild$[pos]$ $= 1$, the bit position of the first child node is calculated by $\mathbf{D-ChildNodePos}(pos) = 256 \times \text{rank}_1(\text{D-HasChild}, pos)$.
- **Move Up**: The bit position of the parent node is computed as $\mathbf{D-ParentNodePos}(pos) = 256 \times \text{select}_1\left(\text{D-HasChild}, \lfloor \frac{pos}{256} \rfloor\right)$.
- **Access Values**: When D-HasChild$[pos]$ $= 0$, the lookup position is given by

$\mathbf{D - ValuePos}(pos) = \text{rank}_1(\text{D-Labels}, pos) - \text{rank}_1(\text{D-HasChild}, pos) + \text{rank}_1(\text{D-IsPrefixKey}, \lfloor \frac{pos}{256} \rfloor) - 1$.

5.2.1.3 LOUDS-Sparse

Compared to LOUDS-Dense, LOUDS-Sparse offers higher space efficiency but with poorer lookup performance. It's better suited for lower levels within a trie structure. The main approach involves using 4 byte or bit sequences to represent trie nodes:

- S-Labels: All branch labels are recorded in level order, and the prefix marked as 0xFF ($) signifies a key node.
- S-HasChild: Indicates whether each branch has child nodes.
- S-LOUDS: Record whether each label is the first label of its node.
- S-Values: Stores node values of fixed size, similar to D-Values in LOUDS-Dense.

Let's take the lower portion of Fig. 5.5 as an illustration. At the second level, the initial non-value node branches out three times. The S-Labels array stores the labels of these branches in order: $, **t**, and **g**. In the SuRF structure, a special byte 0xFF, represented as $, serves a unique purpose. When this byte is placed as the first byte of a node, it signals that the prefix leading to that node is a valid key in itself. Thanks to its fixed position at the start of each node, this special byte can be easily told apart from regular 0xFF labels that might appear elsewhere.

Looking at the example's lower part, among the three branches of the second-level non-value node, only the branch labeled **t** descends to a sub-trie. As a result, in the S-HasChild bitvector, the bit corresponding to **t** is set to 1, while the others remain 0. Regarding the S-LOUDS encoding, which is used to represent the tree structure efficiently, the same second-level non-value node with three branches is encoded as the bit sequence 100. This encoding helps in navigating the tree structure effectively.

Tree navigation on LOUDS-Sparse is as follows:

- **Move Down**: To determine the position of the child node, use the formula $\mathbf{S - ChildNodePos}(pos) = \text{select}_1(\text{S-LOUDS}, \text{rank}_1(\text{S-HasChild}, pos) + 1)$.
- **Move Up**: To find the position of the parent node, apply the formula $\mathbf{S - ParentNodePos}(pos) = \text{select}_1(\text{S-HasChild}, \text{rank}_1(\text{S-LOUDS}, pos) - 1)$.
- **Access Values**: To access the values, utilize the formula $\mathbf{S - ValuePos}(pos) = pos - \text{rank}_1(\text{S-HasChild}, pos) - 1$.

5.2.1.4 SuRF

SuRF's underlying principle is to trim and restructure the FST. It does so by eliminating nodes at the lower levels and substituting them with suffix bits of keywords. This approach aims at achieving a balance between maintaining a low

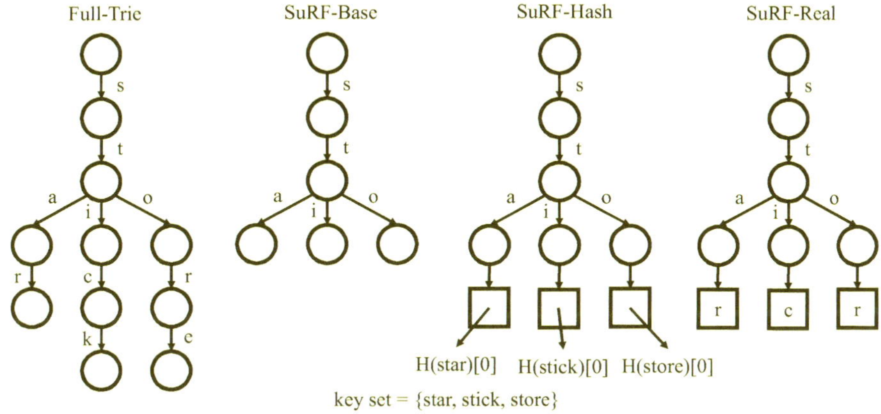

Fig. 5.6 Example of deriving SuRF variations from a full trie

FPR and optimizing the memory usage of the filter. In this context, we present four different versions of SuRF.

The SuRF Basic version (SuRF-Base) stores the shortest key prefixes needed for unique key identification. Taking an example of Fig. 5.6, instead of storing the full keys as "star," "stick," and "store," SuRF-Base truncates the entire trie by including only the shared prefix "st" and one more byte as "a," "i," and "o" for each key. This approach significantly saves space, but at the cost of reduced precision, leading to potential false positives. This is due to the possibility of nonexistent key coincidentally matching stored key prefixes. In order to decrease FPR , three additional variants were devised:

- **SuRF-Hash**: This variant enhances SuRF-Base by appending a small number of hash bits per key, which helps reduce the FPR. When retrieving a keyword, comparisons are performed not only within the trie structure but also against the stored hash value. This design significantly improves the efficiency of point queries. However, it does not provide any direct support for range queries.
- **SuRF-Real**: In this version, the n key bits immediately following the stored prefix of a key are directly stored as the suffix. While this approach does improve the FPR for both point and range queries, it introduces a trade-off. Using real key bits for the suffix does not achieve as low an FPR as using hashed bits. This is because the distribution correlation between stored keys and query keys weakens the distinguishability of real suffix bits.
- **SuRF-Mixed**: This is a hybrid approach that combines both hashed and real key suffix bits. For identical keys, their suffix bits are stored contiguously, enabling the retrieval of both types of suffix with a single-memory access. The lengths of both the hashed and real suffixes can be adjusted to optimize performance based on specific use cases.

5.2.2 *Operation: Search and Query*

LOUDS-DS efficiently supports three fundamental operations:

- **ExactKeySearch**(key): Returns the value associated with the given key if it exists; otherwise, returns NULL.
- **LowerBound**(key): Returns an iterator pointing to the key-value pair (k, v) where k is the smallest key in lexicographical order that is greater than or equal to the input key key.
- **MoveToNext**($iter$): Advances the iterator to the next key-value pair in the lexicographical order.

Point queries in LOUDS-DS start by searching the LOUDS-Dense layer. If the target key is not found there, the search continues in the LOUDS-Sparse layer. The high-level search process is independent of the encoding mechanism and proceeds as follows: first, the target key byte is sought within the label sequence of the current node. If the byte is absent, the search terminates, returning NULL. If found, the corresponding HasChild bit is checked. A value of 1 indicates the branch has child nodes, leading to the computation of the starting position of the child nodes in the label sequence and advancement to the next layer. A value of 0 indicates the branch terminates at a leaf, prompting the return of the corresponding value from the value sequence. Two aggregate values are precomputed based on the LOUDS-Dense layer: the total number of nodes and the count of HasChild bits set to 1. These precomputed values enable the LOUDS-Sparse layer to operate as if the entire tree were encoded using the LOUDS-Sparse format.

Range queries in LOUDS-DS employ a high-level algorithm similar to that of point queries. During a LowerBound operation, instead of an exact match, the algorithm looks for the smallest label that is lexicographically greater than the target label. When moving to the next key, the iterator starts from the current leaf label position and proceeds forward. If another valid label l is found within the node, the algorithm navigates to the leftmost leaf node in the subtree rooted at l. If the iterator reaches the node boundary, it backtracks to the corresponding position in the parent node.

Next, we will introduce how SuRF implements its basic operations using a FST:

- **Lookup Operation**: The **lookup**(k) function determines if a key k might exist in the structure. It returns *true* if k could be present (which may be a false positive) and *false* if k is definitely not present. The lookup process terminates early with a *false* result if the search concludes before reaching a leaf node. For SuRF-Base, reaching a leaf node automatically returns *true*. In other SuRF variants, when a leaf is reached, the stored key suffix k_s is retrieved from the leaf and compared with the corresponding suffix bits extracted from k. The result of this comparison determines the final return value.
- **MoveToNext Operation**: The **MoveToNext**(k) function returns an iterator pointing to the smallest key that is lexicographically greater than or equal to k. This is achieved through a lower-bound search on the FST, which navigates to

a leaf node. If the search encounters an approximated key (prefix without exact suffix match), the fp_{flag} is set to *false*, indicating a potential false positive, and the current iterator is returned. If the prefix of k matches a stored key k' in the trie:

- SuRF-Base and SuRF-Hash lack additional suffix bits to determine the order between k and k', so they set fp_{flag} to *true* and return the iterator pointing to k'.
- SuRF-Real and SuRF-Mixed compare the stored suffix bits k'_r of k' with the suffix bits k_r of k:

  If $k'_r > k_r$, set fp_{flag} to *false* and return the current iterator.
  If $k'_r = k_r$, set fp_{flag} to *true* and return the current iterator.
  If $k'_r < k_r$, set fp_{flag} to *false* and return the iterator advanced to the next key.

- **Count Operation**: The **count**$(lowKey, highKey)$ function returns the number of keys within the range $[lowKey, highKey]$. It also sets low_fp_{flag} and $high\_fp_{flag}$ to indicate potential over-counting at the range boundaries. The operation starts by calling **MoveToNext**$(lowKey)$ and sets low_fp_{flag} if necessary. The iterator is then advanced, incrementing the count until the key k' pointed to by the iterator is greater than or equal to $highKey$. If k' matches the prefix of $highKey$, $high\_fp_{flag}$ is set to indicate a possible false positive at the upper boundary.

5.2.3 Analysis: LOUDS-DS and Space

As previously discussed, LOUDS-Dense trades off encoding efficiency to enhance query performance. Additionally, the size of LOUDS-Dense is constrained by the ratio R to prevent it from compromising the overall space efficiency of LOUDS-DS. Consider a trie with H levels, where $LOUDS-Dense-Size(l)$ denotes the space occupied by LOUDS-Dense encoding from level 0 up to (but not including) level l, and $LOUDS-Sparse-Size(l)$ represents the space used by LOUDS-Sparse encoding from level l to level H. The cutoff level is defined as the maximum l satisfying $LOUDS-Dense-Size(l) \times R \leq LOUDS-Sparse-Size(l)$, with R set to 64 by default. It is important to note that LOUDS-Dense does not always require more space than LOUDS-Sparse; when a node's branching factor exceeds 51, LOUDS-Dense demands fewer bits for representation. Given the prevalence of such nodes in the upper levels of a trie, integrating LOUDS-Dense often improves space efficiency compared to using LOUDS-Sparse alone.

Furthermore, the encoding size of LOUDS-Sparse determines the actual space usage of the trie. For a trie with n nodes, LOUDS-Sparse consumes $10n$ bits: $8n$ bits for S-Labels, n bits for S-HasChild, and n bits for S-LOUDS. According to information theory, the lower bound is approximately $9.44n$ bits. Although LOUDS-

Sparse approaches this lower bound, it is classified as compact rather than succinct in fine-grained taxonomies, as it requires $O(Z)$ space instead of $Z + o(Z)$. Notably, the FST is smaller than any other succinct trie structure.

5.3 Robust Space-Time Optimized Range Filter (Rosetta)

The Robust Space-Time Optimized Range Filter (Rosetta) [3] is a range filter designed for LSM-tree-based key-value stores. Its core innovation lies in strategically trading increased filter probe latency for significantly improved false positive rates. Rosetta decomposes each range query into multiple nonoverlapping binary prefix probes, leveraging a hierarchy of Bloom filter indices that collectively cover all key prefixes. The filter dynamically adapts to workload patterns by modifying the cardinality of active Bloom filters and then reallocating memory across the hierarchy. This space-time optimization enables Rosetta to continuously balance FPR against computational overhead during LSM-tree operations.

5.3.1 Structure: Stacked Bloom Filters

Rosetta implements a stacked Bloom filter architecture, where each filter corresponds to a distinct binary prefix length of the stored keys. For every key in the LSM-tree, Rosetta constructs indexes for all possible prefixes, hashing each prefix into its respective Bloom filter to enable efficient prefix-based range queries. This design effectively constructs an implicit Segment Tree structure over the filters. By leveraging the complete binary tree property of Segment Trees, where node relationships are determined solely by their positions, Rosetta avoids explicit child pointer storage, achieving optimal space efficiency.

Taking the example of Fig. 5.7, when inserting the key 7 (corresponding to 0111), all its prefixes—0, 01, 011, and 0111—are added to the first, second, third, and fourth Bloom filters, respectively. Notably, a range query with size R is broken down into at most $2\log_2(R)$ dyadic intervals. (A dyadic interval refers to an interval whose boundaries align with powers of 2.)

As illustrated in Fig. 5.7, the bottom layer of Rosetta indexes the full prefix of each key, equal to indexing the entire key in a traditional Bloom filter—a design default in LSM-trees to prevent point queries from triggering unnecessary disk accesses. Rosetta demonstrates high efficiency in processing point queries, matching the performance of LSM-trees optimized specifically for such operations. When executing a point query on any run of the LSM-tree, the system first consults only the last layer of the corresponding Rosetta instance. A disk access is initiated only if this interaction with Rosetta yields a positive result.

Rosetta's core design mechanism converts range queries into a sequence of prefix queries, which are subsequently transformed into point queries. This methodology

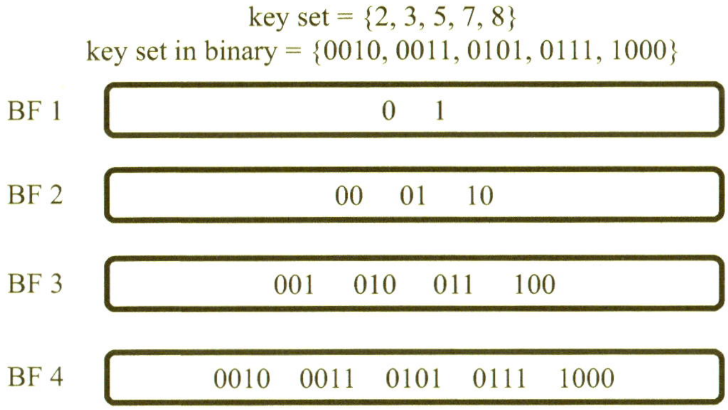

Fig. 5.7 Rosetta constructs indexes for all prefixes of each key

boosts Rosetta's efficiency in processing range queries, enabling it to swiftly identify and validate query boundaries.

5.3.2 Operation: Insert and Range Query

Rosetta is instantiated either when data from the memory buffer is flushed to persistent storage or when two or more older runs are consolidated into a new run. Consequently, Rosetta requires only a single insertion process once all keys are known. Moreover, within the dynamic operations of an LSM-tree, each run may contain a distinct set of keys. This inherent variability implies that different Rosetta instances can have varying numbers of Bloom filters.

As illustrated in Algorithm 24, the insertion procedure decomposes keys into binary prefixes of varying lengths, producing $\mathcal{L}$ distinct prefixes for a key with $\mathcal{L}$ bits. These prefixes are then inserted into the corresponding Bloom filters of Rosetta, denoted as $\mathcal{B}_i$.

Using the example in Fig. 5.7, inserting the key 7 (represented as 0111 in binary) involves inserting its prefixes 0, 01, 011, and 0111 into $\mathcal{B}_1$, $\mathcal{B}_2$, $\mathcal{B}_3$, and

Algorithm 24 Rosetta insertion

```
function InsertKey( key )
    bitLength ← the binary length of key
    bloomFilters ← Bloom Filter arraies with the size of bitLength
    for i = bitLength down to 1 do
        bloomFilters[i].insert (key)
        key ← ⌊key/2⌋
    end for
end function
```

Algorithm 25 Rosetta range query

```
function RANGEQUERY(Low, High, P = 0, l = 1)
    //[Low, High] : the query range
    //P: the prefix
    if P > High or P + 2^(L−l+1) − 1 < Low then
        //P is not contained in the range
        return false
    end if
    if P ≥ Low and P + 2^(L−l+1) − 1 ≤ High then
        //P is contained in the range
        return DOUBT(P, l)
    end if
    if RANGEQUERY(Low, High, P, l + 1) then
        return true
    end if
    return RANGEQUERY(Low, High, P + 2^(L−l), l + 1)
end function
function DOUBT(P, l)
    if ¬B_l.POINTQUERY(P) then
        return false
    end if
    if l > L then
        return true
    end if
    if DOUBT(P, l + 1) then
        return true
    end if
    return DOUBT(P + 2^(L−l), l + 1)
end function
```

$\mathcal{B}_4$, respectively. Importantly, similar to conventional Bloom filters, this insertion process indexes each prefix by hashing and setting the corresponding bits within the filters.

Algorithm 25 illustrates the execution of range queries in Rosetta. First, the specified key range is broken down into multiple dyadic intervals, each corresponding to distinct sub-trees that comprehensively index all keys within the interval. For each dyadic interval, the initial step involves identifying the specific prefix that encompasses all keys in the interval. Take Fig. 5.8 as an example: the range [7, 11] decomposes into two dyadic intervals—[7, 7] and [8, 11]. In Rosetta's design, the Segment Tree operates implicitly, making the prefix length critical for determining which Bloom filter to probe. For instance, the prefix "10*" includes all keys in [8, 11], so we probe the prefix "10" in the second Bloom filter for this range. If all probes for the dyadic intervals return negative, the query range is empty.

When at least one probe returns positive, Rosetta initiates the doubting process: delving into deeper sub-trees to probe Bloom filters at lower levels and validate the actual existence of corresponding prefixes. Continuing the example in Fig. 5.8, a positive probe for "10*" triggers further probing of "100*" and "101*" in the third Bloom filter. Notably, if both deeper probes return negative, the subrange is

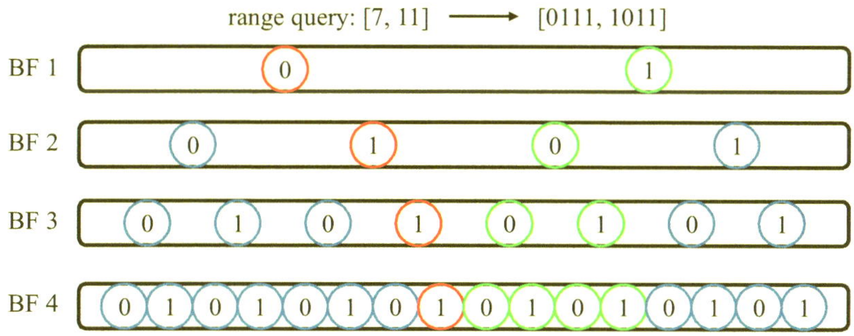

Fig. 5.8 Rosetta utilizes recursive prefix probing

marked empty—any key with prefix "10*" must have either "100*" or "101*" as its extended prefix.

Rosetta employs a recursive layer-by-layer probing of Bloom filters, verifying the existence of intermediate prefixes through pre-order traversal of both left and right subtrees. The left subtree is formed by appending 0 to the current prefix, while the right subtree is constructed by appending 1. The recursive traversal of a subtree terminates in two scenarios:

- When probing a Bloom filter corresponding to a left-leaf node of the subtree yields a positive result, classifying the entire subrange as positive
- If any probe related to a right-side node returns a negative result, categorizing the entire subrange as negative

As previously mentioned, the bottom level of Rosetta indexes the complete prefix of each key. Therefore, for point queries, the procedure involves solely inspecting the bottom level of Rosetta for the current run.

5.3.3 Analysis: Space and Construction Time

We define the following terms and notation:

- n : Total number of keys in the dataset.
- R : Maximum size of a range query (in terms of key count).
- M : Total memory budget allocated for the filter structure.
- $\mathcal{B}_i$: Bloom filter instance corresponding to prefixes of length i.
- ϵ_i: FPR of the i-th Bloom filter Bi.
- M_i: Memory space allocated specifically to Bloom filter Bi.
- ϵ: Aggregate FPR for prefix queries after recursive probing.
- $\emptyset$: Notation denoting the general FPR characteristic of Bloom filters in Rosetta's architecture.

5.3.3.1 Space Complexity

Previous research shows that any data structure needs at least $nlog\left(\frac{R^{1-O(\epsilon)}}{\epsilon}\right) - O(n)$ bits to ensure a FPR of ϵ for any range query with size R.

Rosetta utilizes several approaches to optimize memory allocation. An initial solution involves establishing an equilibrium where each node u maintains a consistent FPR, designated as ϵ. This is achieved by taking into account the filters at node u as well as those at its descendant nodes. Delving into the specifics, the calculation of the FPR $\emptyset$ for the filter at node u's level unfolds as follows: we assume that each child of node u achieves a FPR of ϵ, which is reflective of the filters at their descendant nodes. When we collectively examine the filters of u and its descendants, the eventual false positive emerges from two potential scenarios:

- The filter at node u returns positive, coupled with positive return from u's left sub-tree, thus leading to a positive rate of $\emptyset \cdot \epsilon$.
- A positive result from the filter at node u is countered by a negative result from its left subtree, whereas the right subtree of u yields a positive result. This scenario results in a calculated positive rate of $\emptyset \cdot (1 - \epsilon) \cdot \epsilon$.

Integrating both cases yields the subsequent equation:

$$\emptyset \cdot \epsilon + \emptyset \cdot (1 - \epsilon) \cdot \epsilon = \epsilon \Rightarrow \emptyset = \frac{1}{2-\epsilon}$$

Consequently, it is feasible to assign a FPR of $\frac{1}{2-\epsilon}$ to each intermediate node.

The first-cut solution results in an ϵ FPR at last level, but a $\frac{1}{2-\epsilon}$ FPR for preceding levels. Given that each level in Rosetta can contain up to n nodes, the total memory requirement is expressed as

$$loge \cdot (nlog\left(\frac{1}{\epsilon}\right) + nlog(u)log(2 - \epsilon)) \approx 1.44 \cdot nlog\left(\frac{u}{\epsilon}\right)$$

where u denotes the key space size. In scenarios with a maximum range query size R, several levels of Rosetta can be disregarded, leading to a reduced memory usage of $1.44 \cdot nlog\left(\frac{R}{\epsilon}\right)$, which is close to the theoretical lower bound.

5.3.3.2 Computational Complexity

Regarding the operations of Rosetta, we analyze the computational complexity of its construction and execution of queries.

Given the key-sorted nature of LSM-tree runs, Rosetta streamlines prefix insertion by removing redundant storage of shared prefixes among consecutive keys. This approach guarantees that only unique prefixes are added to the Bloom filter hierarchy. Consequently, the total number of insertions into the Bloom filters corresponds to the size of a trie housing these keys. This size is restricted by $n \cdot \mathcal{L}$, a complexity that closely approaches the theoretical lower bound. Achieving this bound necessitates minimal processing, mainly just reading each bit of the keys.

The time complexity of a query is directly proportional to the maximum number of prefixes into which the range is decomposed. In the worst case, the number of probes required for a range query equals the number of Segment Tree nodes corresponding to each binary range, which is $O(R)$. However, recursion often terminates in advance; thus, the number of probes is typically much less than the worst case. We discuss this in two scenarios.

The first scenario is uniform bits-allocation, which means every Bloom filter's FPR equals $p = 0.5 + \theta, 0 < |\theta| < 0.5$. The expected query runtime for an empty range is bounded by $O\left(\frac{\log R}{\theta^2}\right)$. For empty range scenarios, the doubting process is categorized by whether it reaches recursively to the bottom level of Rosetta. Let E denote the number of probes that terminate before reaching the bottom level, and F denote those that reach the bottom level (i.e., level $\mathcal{L}$). Consequently, the total number of probes is $E + F$, for which we analyze the upper bound. Consider a hypothetical Rosetta instance with infinitely many Bloom filters, each exhibiting a FPR of p. The computational complexity of this new Rosetta is not less than the original: if the query does not reach level $\mathcal{L}$, or if probes at layer $\mathcal{L}$ always return negative, then both have the same probing cost. However, if the query at layer $\mathcal{L}$ returns positive, the new Rosetta will continue to recurse, leading to increased probing costs.

Let E_i represent the number of probes with i positive Bloom filter detections; thus, $\sum_{i=0}^{\infty} E_i = E$. Each positive probe can recurse into three scenarios: two negative probes, two positive probes, one negative probe, and one positive probe. Therefore, all probes form a binary tree where the leaf nodes are negative probes, and the intermediate nodes are positive probes. This means there are a total of $i + 1$ negatives and i positive detections, adding up to $2i + 1$ probes. Further, we have $E_i = P_i(2_i + 1)$, where P_i denotes the probability that the number of positive probes equals i. Let C_i signify the i-th Catalan number, defined as the quantity of distinct binary trees featuring $2i + 1$ nodes. Thus, $P_i = C_i \cdot p_i \cdot (1 - p)^{i+1}$. By the approximation C_i is $\frac{4^i}{i^{\frac{3}{2}}\sqrt{\pi}}$, we have that

$$P_i \approx \frac{(1 - 4\theta^2)^i}{i\sqrt{i\pi}} \cdot (1 - p) \le \frac{(1 - 4\theta^2)^i}{i\sqrt{i\pi}}$$

$$\Longrightarrow E_i = P_i(2i + 1) \le \frac{(1 - 4\theta^2)^i (2i + 1)}{i\sqrt{i\pi}}$$

$$\Longrightarrow E - E_0 = \sum_{i=1}^{\infty} E_i \le \sum_{i=1}^{\infty} \frac{(1 - 4\theta^2)^i (2i + 1)}{i\sqrt{i\pi}}$$

$$\le \sum_{i=1}^{\infty} \frac{3i(1 - 4\theta^2)^i}{i\sqrt{i\pi}} \le \sum_{i=1}^{\infty} \frac{3(1 - 4\theta^2)^i}{\sqrt{\pi}} \le \frac{3}{4\theta^2\sqrt{\pi}}$$

Since E_0 is a constant and we have at most $2logR$ dyadic intervals, the probe cost to be at most $O\left(\frac{logR}{\theta^2}\right)$. So for the original Rosetta, a range query's expected complexity is less than $O\left(\frac{logR}{\theta^2}\right)$.

The second scenario involves nonuniform bit allocation, allowing Bloom filters to have differing FPRs. Let p_i denote the FPR of the i-th level Bloom filter, with $p_{\max} = \max\{p_i\}$ and $p_{\min} = \min\{p_i\}$. Similar to the uniform case, we derive

$$P_i \leq C_i p_{\max}^i (1 - p_{\min})^{i+1}$$

where C_i is the i-th Catalan number (counting the number of distinct binary trees with $2i + 1$ nodes). This approximates to $\frac{4^i}{i^{3/2}\sqrt{\pi}} (p_{\max}(1 - p_{\min}))^i (1 - p_{\min})$.

To maintain the same complexity analysis as in the uniform FPR scenario, we require $p_{\max}(1 - p_{\min}) < 1/4$, and $\theta' = \sqrt{1/4 - p_{\max}(1 - p_{\min})}$, the expected probe complexity becomes $O\left(\frac{\log R}{\theta'2}\right)$.

5.4 Bloom Range Filter (BloomRF)

BloomRF [4] is another range filter. The design synergistically integrates Bloom filters with prefix-based hashing, where range information is encoded directly within key-derived hash codes. A key innovation is the piecewise-monotone hash function (PMHF), which preserves local key ordering while reducing memory access frequency during range queries. This dual capability, efficient point lookup and range probing, enables BloomRF to achieve robust performance across diverse query workloads.

Compared to previously mentioned range filters like ARF, SuRF, and Rosetta, BloomRF addresses three major pain points. Firstly, previous range filters were optimized for handling different query range sizes, while BloomRF stands out with its constant query complexity, which remains unaffected by the size of the query range. Secondly, in contrast to the existing range filters that are offline, BloomRF operates online. This means that BloomRF can handle queries concurrently with data insertions, enhancing its applicability and efficiency. Lastly, while previous range filters are vulnerable to data and workload skew, BloomRF demonstrates robust performance, showing resilience against such skewness in data and workload distributions, ensuring reliable and consistent query results.

5.4.1 Structure: Bloom Filter with Dyadic Intervals

Dyadic intervals can be structured across dyadic levels, where a level-l interval contains 2^l keys. In a domain represented by d bits, there exist $d + 1$ dyadic levels

$\ell \in \{0, 1, ..., d\}$. Each level-$l$ dyadic interval decomposes into two level-($l - 1$) dyadic intervals. For example, the level-1 interval [0, 1] splits into [0, 0] and [1, 1] at level 0.

Let $code(y)$ denote the bit array sequence (with m bits) generated by k hash functions in Bloom filters:

$$code(y) = (h_{k-1}(y), h_{k-2}(y), \ldots, h_0(y))$$

and $code(y)_i$ represents the i-th layer prefix of $code(y)$, which is the ordered sequence of the first $k - i$ hash-function outputs in $code(y)$:

$$code(y)_i = (h_{k-1}(y), h_{k-2}(y), \ldots, h_i(y))$$

Additionally, a level-l prefix of y is defined as the sequence of $d - l$ most significant bits of y, assuming y is encoded with d bits. Importantly, level-l prefixes correspond to level-l dyadic intervals.

5.4.1.1 Prefix Hashing

The core principle of prefix hashing is to embed range information directly within the $code(y)$ structure. Notably, while $code(y)$ consists of only k hash functions, the domain spans $d + 1$ dyadic levels, necessitating a selection of specific levels $\ell_{k-1} \geq \ell_{k-2} \geq \cdots \geq \ell_0$. Prefix hashing mandates that a dyadic level-ℓ_i prefix of y corresponds to a layer-i prefix of $code(y)$. Formally, for any keys y and y',

$$y \gg \ell_i = y' \gg \ell_i \implies code(y)_i = code(y')_i$$

To ensure this property holds for arbitrary hash functions, the hash functions in $code(y)_i$ operate exclusively on prefixes of level $\geq \ell_i$:

$$code(y) = \big(h_{k-1}(y \gg \ell_{k-1}),\ h_{k-2}(y \gg \ell_{k-2}),\ \ldots,\ h_0(y \gg \ell_0)\big)$$

Thus, $code(y)$ effectively tests whether a dyadic interval at level ℓ_i contains the target key. By associating each dyadic interval with $code(y)_i$, BloomRF implicitly encodes range information within $code(y)$.

Finally, we determine the levels ℓ_i and the number of hash functions k. Equidistant levels offer a practical and intuitive solution. Setting Δ as the uniform spacing between consecutive levels, each level is defined as $\ell_i = i\Delta$. The value of k is derived as $\lceil (d+1)/\Delta \rceil$. However, accounting for saturation in the top layers due to key density, we refine this to $k = \lceil (d - \log_2 n)/\Delta \rceil$, where n denotes the number of keys.

Let's take the key set $\{13, 58, 1447\}$ within a 16-bit domain as an example. We'll set Δ to 4, the bit-array length m to 30 bits, and calculate k as $\lceil (d - \log_2 n)/\Delta \rceil$,

Table 5.1 Layers i, levels l_i, and parameters for the hash functions

Layer i	3	2	1	0
Level l_i	12	8	4	0
a_i	2	3	5	7
b_i	29	31	37	41

Key	h_3	h_2	h_1	h_0
13	2	3	5	0
58	2	3	26	15
1447	2	8	5	24

bit array: 1011 0100 1000 0001 0000 0000 1010 0000

Fig. 5.9 Example of prefix hashing

which results in 4. The hash function we'll use is defined as

$$h_i(x) = a_i + b_i(x \gg \ell_i) \mod m$$

The parameters for the hash functions, along with the corresponding layers i and levels l_i, are presented in Table 5.1. Figure 5.9 displays the prefix hashing codes of all the keys and the bit-array after all keys have been inserted.

For the key 13, its code for the positions in the bit array is (2, 3, 5, 0). Prefix hashing enables us to utilize $code(y)$ to verify if the dyadic intervals at level l_i contain the target key (in this case, 13). All keys y within the range [0, 15] share the prefix $0x000$ at level l_1. As a result, they all have the same $code(y)_1$ value of (2, 3, 5). By checking the positions (2, 3, 5) in the bit-array, we can perform a range query for the interval [0, 15], and the result is positive, indicating the presence of the key 13.

5.4.1.2 Piecewise-Monotone Hash Functions(PMHF)

While prefix hashing ensures efficient space utilization, the hash functions themselves do not guarantee the maintenance of local order for prefixes $y >> \ell_i$. As a result, interval lookups require accessing more memory, which diminishes performance efficiency. To address this, piecewise-monotone hash functions are proposed to ensure that encoded adjacent keys yield neighboring hash values, thus enabling faster interval lookups. Any hash function h_i can be adapted to satisfy this characteristic with computational efficiency through

$$\Big((h_i(x >> (\Delta - 1)) \mod \frac{m}{2^{\Delta-1}}) << (\Delta - 1)\Big) + x \,\&\, (2^{\Delta} - 1)$$

Key	MH_3	MH_2	MH_1	MH_0
13	16	24	8	5
58	16	24	11	18
1447	16	29	2	31

BloomRF	0010 0100 1001 0000 1010 0000 1000 0101

Fig. 5.10 Example of PMHF

Here, x is right-shifted by $\Delta - 1$ bits, restricting h to operate on the remaining bits. Additionally, bit-array access is performed in word sizes of $2^{\Delta-1}$, requiring m to be a multiple of this value. The hash value is then left-shifted by $\Delta - 1$ bits and combined with the least significant $\Delta - 1$ bits, preserving the order of these bits in the prefix. Integrating with prefix hashing, we define

$$MH_i(x) = \left(\left(h_i\big(x >> (\ell_i + \Delta - 1)\big) \bmod \frac{m}{2^{\Delta-1}}\right) << (\Delta - 1)\right) + \big(x >> \ell_i\big) \;\&\; (2^{\Delta} - 1)$$

Continuing with the key set $\{13, 58, 1447\}$, we again set $\Delta = 4$, $k = 4$, and $m = 32$. Using $h_i(x) = a_i + b_i x$ for hashing, the corresponding parameters are detailed in Table 5.1.

Figure 5.10 shows the PMHF codes for keys and the bit-array after inserting all keys.

To assess the dyadic interval $[13, 14]$, one must verify the codes $(16, 24, 8, 5)$ and $(16, 24, 8, 6)$. These codes share identical prefixes across levels 3 to 1, with adjacent positions 5 and 6 at level 0—allowing single-word access for the test. The level-0 positions 5 and 6 are represented by the bit mask $b = 0b00000110$. Accessing the first byte of the bit-array returns $w = 0b00100100$. With bits set at positions 16, 24, and 8, and since $b \;\&\; w \neq 0$, the test yields a positive result.

5.4.2 *Operation: Insert and Range Query*

We are now set to delve into a comprehensive exposition of bloomRF's principal operations, encompassing insertion, and conducting point or range queries.

For insertion and point query operations in BloomRF, the process starts with calculating the $code(x)$ of bit-array positions for a key x using piecewise-monotone hash-functions $MH_i(x)$, where i iterates from $k - 1$ to 0. The corresponding bits in the bit-array are then marked as 1. To determine whether a query key y exists in the set, BloomRF computes $code(y)$ similarly and checks if all corresponding bits in the bit-array are marked.

Range queries function by decomposing arbitrary lookup intervals I into dyadic intervals. This decomposition employs a two-path algorithm tailored for the left and right boundaries of I. The process initiates from the top level, with J_d encompassing I, and proceeds recursively: if $J_{\ell+1}$ ($\ell < d$) covers I, it splits into two dyadic intervals K^l and K^r, and J_ℓ is set to the interval covering I. When I is not contained within a single dyadic interval, the path branches into two: $J_\ell^l = K^l$ for the left boundary and $J_l^r = K^r$ for the right boundary.

Considering the symmetry, we focus on describing the dyadic intervals for the left path in BloomRF. Suppose $J_{\ell+1}^l$ ($\ell < d$) encompasses the left boundary of I, and we decompose $J_{\ell+1}^l$ into K^l and K^r. If K^l overlaps with I and K^r is completely contained within I, then $I_\ell^l = K^r$ becomes part of I's dyadic interval decomposition, and $J_\ell^l = K^l$ covers I's left boundary. Conversely, if K^r does not fully overlap with I, K^r assumes the role of covering the left boundary, setting $J_\ell^l = K^r$. Otherwise, the decomposition finalizes with $I_\ell^l = K^r$.

Take the example in Fig. 5.11: for $I = [33, 48]$, the decomposition yields $I_0^l \cup I_1^l \cup I_2^l \cup I_3^l \cup I_0^r = [33, 33] \cup [34, 35] \cup [36, 39] \cup [40, 47] \cup [48, 48]$, which are the intervals to be probed.

Range queries follow Algorithm 26, traversing layers from the top ($i = k - 1$) to the bottom ($i = 0$). At each layer, it uses PMHF MH_i to conduct key tests on coverings ($J_{\ell i}$) and decomposed intervals of I (represented as unions $I_{\ell i}$). The "checks" variable stores critical data: $check.l_key$, $check.r_key$, and $check.is_covering$. When encountering a covering, the algorithm simplifies to a single bit test: if the bit is set, it proceeds to compute checks for the next layer; otherwise, it concludes the interval is empty, avoiding deeper checks. For decomposed intervals, it computes a bit mask b—thanks to PMHF, all relevant bits are accessed in a single word. A bitwise AND

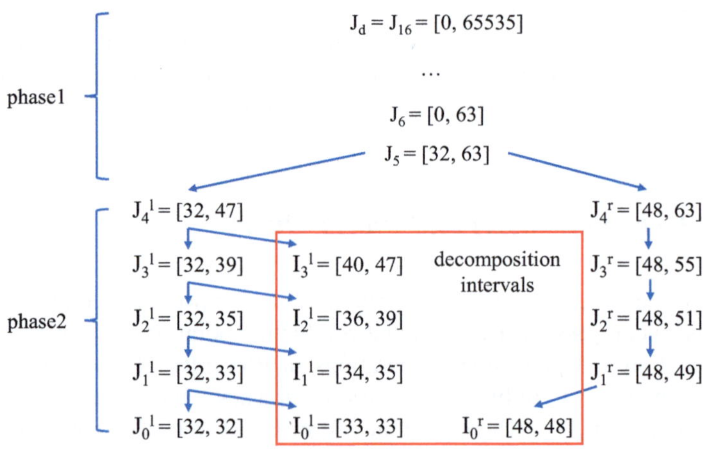

Fig. 5.11 Dyadic intervals for range [33, 48]

Algorithm 26 BloomRF range lookup

```
function RANGELOOKUP(l_key, r_key)
    Let i ← k − 1;
    Let checks ← init_checks(l_key, r_key, i);
    while checks ≠ ∅ do
        Let new_checks ← ∅
        for check ∈ checks do
            if checks.is_covering = true then
                if filter.bit_access(MH_i(check.l_key)) = 1 then
                    Expand check to layer i − 1 an append to new_checks;
                end if
            else
                Let b ← bit_mask(check.l_key, check.r_key);
                Let w ← filter.word_access(MH_i(check.l_key));
                if b & w ≠ 0 then
                    return true;
                end if
            end if
        end for
        Let i ← i − 1;
        Let checks ← new_checks;
    end while
    return false;
end function
```

operation on b and the word returns nonzero if keys are present, yielding a positive result. If all decomposed intervals are excluded, BloomRF returns negative.

5.4.3 Analysis: Time and FPR

BloomRF achieves near-optimal space efficiency because $code(y)$ inherently encodes range information via corresponding dyadic intervals. Specifically, prefix hashing compresses the difference between consecutive key prefixes into one bit stored at a fixed array position.

For time complexity analysis of the operations: insertion and point queries each involve evaluating k hash functions, resulting in constant time complexity $O(k)$. Range queries, governed by Algorithm 26, feature a two-loop structure: an outer loop iterating over layers and an inner loop processing checks per layer. With k layers and at most four word-accesses per layer, range query complexity also remains constant at $O(k)$.

To estimate FPR ϵ for range queries: as illustrated in Fig. 5.11, an arbitrary interval I decomposes into dyadic intervals. The framework categorizes cases based on I's position:

1. Phase 1: i_1 coverings by single dyadic intervals J_{ℓ_i} for $j \in [k, k - i_i + 1]$

2. Phase 2: Transitions to i_2 coverings by dyadic interval pairs $J^l_{\ell j} \cup J^r_{\ell j}$ for $j \in [k - i_1, k - i_1 - i_2 + 1]$

   A false positive occurs if:

- All phase 1 dyadic intervals return positive
- All left-side phase 2 intervals return positive while right-side results vary (or vice versa)

Since each interval maps to a single bit, verification simplifies to bit checks. Let p denote the probability of a bit being unset in the bit-array. We have that

$$
\begin{aligned}
\epsilon &\leq (1-p)^{i_1+i_2}\left(2\sum_{i=0}^{i_2-1}\binom{i_2}{i}p^{i_2-i}(1-p)^i + (1-p)^{i_2}\right) \\
&= 2(1-p)^{i_1+i_2}\left(\underbrace{\sum_{i=0}^{i_2}\binom{i_2}{i}p^{i_2-i}(1-p)^i}_{=1} -(1-p)^{i_2}\right) \\
&\leq 2(1-p)^{i_1+i_2}
\end{aligned}
$$

Dyadic intervals situated at level $l_i = i\Delta$ are characterized by a length of $2^{i\Delta}$. Consequently, for any given interval I with a length constraint of $|I| \leq 2^{i\Delta}$, it can be inferred that a maximum of two dyadic intervals at level ℓ_i are sufficient to encompass it. This implication is critical for the process delineated in phase 2, ensuring that at a minimum, layer i is attained. This can be formally expressed as $i_1 + i_2 \geq k - i$. From this relationship, it follows that $\epsilon \leq 2(1-p)^{k-i}$. Hence, we deduce the upper bound of ϵ as $\epsilon \leq 2(1-p)^{k-\log_2(|I|)/\Delta}$. Experiments show that for PHMF the assumption of perfectly random hash functions results in a bit-setting probability of $\frac{1}{m}$ under common data distributions. Thus, $p = \left(1 - \frac{1}{m}\right)^{kn} \approx e^{-\frac{kn}{m}}$. Finally, we have that

$$
\epsilon \leq 2\left(1 - e^{-\frac{kn}{m}}\right)^{k-\log_2(R)/\Delta}
$$

For point queries, it is similar to estimate that $\epsilon \approx \left(1 - e^{-\frac{kn}{m}}\right)^k$ for BloomRF behaving like a Bloom filter.

5.5 Sparse Numerical Array-Based Range Filters (SNARF)

Sparse Numerical Array-Based Range Filters (SNARF) [5] represent a learning-enhanced range filtering framework that integrates data-driven modeling and compression techniques to optimize filtering efficiency. The system approximates the

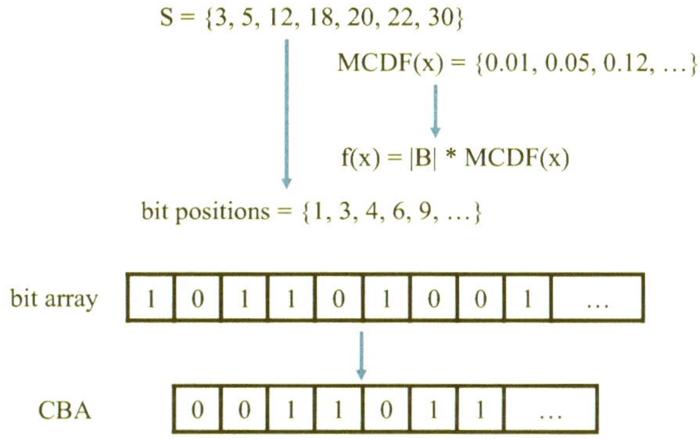

Fig. 5.12 Example SNARF

dataset's cumulative distribution function (CDF) via piecewise linear models, enabling precise key-to-position mapping within a sparse bit array. To minimize storage overhead, SNARF employs high-efficiency compression schemes (e.g., Golomb or Elias-Fano coding) while dynamically adjusting the bit array size to control FPR. By leveraging data distribution characteristics and advanced compression, SNARF achieves superior space-FPR trade-offs compared to prior range filters, without compromising query throughput.

5.5.1 Structure: Range Filter with Linear Model

For a key set $S = \{x_1, x_2, \ldots, x_n\}$, SNARF constructs a cumulative distribution function (CDF) model $MCDF(x)$ to estimate the empirical CDF of the keys. This model is then utilized in the monotonic mapping function $f(x) = \lfloor MCDF(x) \times nK \rfloor$ to map keys into a bit array B with $|B| = n \times K$, where corresponding bits are set to 1. Here, K denotes the scaling factor for the bit array size. Directly storing the entire sparse bit array B is space-inefficient, so SNARF stores a compressed version (CBA, compressed bit array) instead. Figure 5.12 illustrates a simple SNARF example.

5.5.1.1 CDF Model

SNARF uses CDF to map key values into bit arrays to achieve the purpose of distributing keys as evenly as possible throughout the bit array. The CDF used by SNARF is the empirical CDF, which is directly calculated based on the data set. SNARF doesn't use the exact CDF of the dataset, but instead approximates the CDF with a piecewise linear model; the linear model features a compact size and enables rapid numerical evaluation. The detailed procedures are as follows:

1. Uniformly sample specific key values from the dataset as critical reference points.
2. Employ line segments to approximate the CDF between these key points.

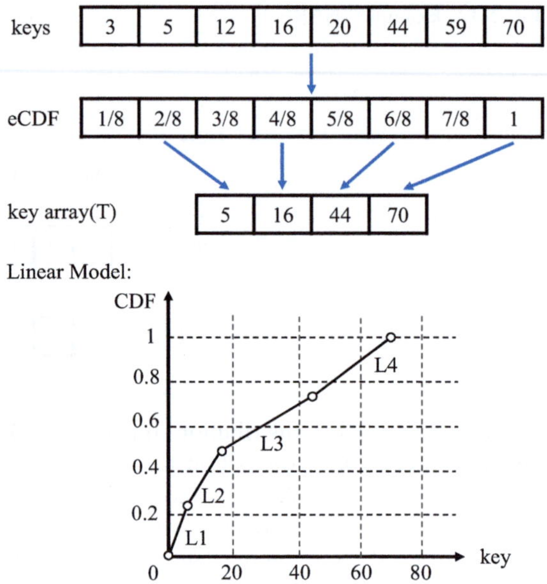

Fig. 5.13 SNARF CDF model

3. Store the slope and intercept of each line segment as model parameters.
4. Based on the position of the query key value, determine the corresponding line segment between two key points, and then use a linear function to quickly estimate its CDF value. It is important to note that if the computed CDF falls outside the [0, 1] range, the value is adjusted to 0 or 1 accordingly (Fig. 5.13).

The effectiveness of CDF model is influenced by the number of line segments employed, and this parameter can be adjusted to optimize the balance between the precision of CDF estimation and the model's overall dimension. Increasing the number of lines enhances the potential accuracy of the CDF approximation, but it also results in a higher space utilization. Empirical evidence suggests that setting the number of line segments to $|S|/1000$ typically achieves a favorable balance between accurate CDF estimation and compact model size. Under this configuration, the model incurs a space consumption of nearly 0.2 bits per key.

5.5.1.2 Compressed Bit Array

SNARF simply encodes the positions of the one bits for compression and implements two compression encoding methods: Golomb coding and Elias-Fano encoding.

Golomb coding processes position values as integers by computing their differences (deltas) and encoding the results. Specifically, a fixed constant M is established, and for each position value X, the quotient $q = \lfloor X/M \rfloor$ and remainder $r = X\%M$ are calculated. The quotient is encoded using unary encoding, while

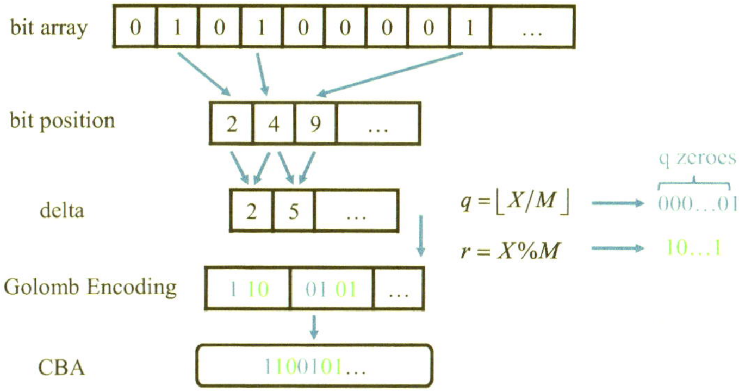

Fig. 5.14 Golomb coding

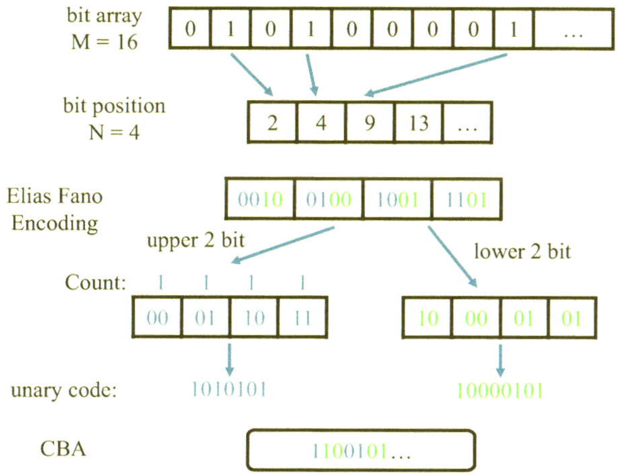

Fig. 5.15 Elias-Fano coding

the remainder is encoded using fixed-length ($\log_2(M)$ bits) binary encoding. An illustration of Golomb encoding with $M = 4$ is provided in Fig. 5.14.

The choice of M significantly impacts the size of the compressed array. For uniformly random values, the optimal constant corresponds to the average delta value, which is derived by dividing the bit array size nK by the number of one bits, n. Consequently, M is set to K (Fig. 5.15).

Elias-Fano encoding partitions a sorted sequence of bit positions into upper and lower bit components. Assuming a universe range $[0, M)$, each position is first represented in binary using $\lceil \log_2(M) \rceil$ bits. For N positions:

- **Lower Bits**: The least significant $\lceil \log_2(M/N) \rceil$ bits are stored verbatim using a simple binary encoding, requiring $N \cdot \lceil \log_2(M/N) \rceil$ bits total.
- **Upper Bits**: The most significant $\lceil \log_2(N) \rceil$ bits are unary-encoded. For each value in $[0, N - 1]$, the count of positions sharing that upper-bit value is represented in unary with a "0" stop bit between values. This requires exactly

$2N$ bits: one "1" bit for each of the N positions plus one "0" bit for each distinct upper value.

The final Elias-Fano representation combines these two encoded components.

In SNARF, the parameters M and N are set to nK and n, respectively. Consequently, each bit position is encoded by binary-encoding the lower $\log_2(K)$ bits and unary-encoding the upper $\log_2(n)$ bits.

When checking for the presence of a 1 bit within the range $[a, b]$, both Golomb coding and Elias-Fano coding require decoding the compressed bit array (CBA) from the start. However, Elias-Fano coding offers an optimization: if the upper bits of a position are less than $\lfloor \frac{a}{2^{M-N}} \rfloor$, the position is guaranteed to be smaller than a because the maximum value of the lower bits is $2^{M-N} - 1$. This property allows skipping the decoding of lower bits when upper bits are irrelevant, reducing memory access during range queries compared to Golomb coding.

To avoid decoding the entire array from the start, SNARF partitions the bit array into equally sized segments of $K\beta$ bits, resulting in n/β segments. For a range query $[p, q]$, only segments overlapping with the range $[f(p), f(q)]$ in the CBA need to be decoded. Specifically, segments from $\lfloor f(p)\beta/n \rfloor$ to $\lfloor f(q)\beta/n \rfloor$ are considered.

While standard rank-select structures, such as those used in SuRF, enable efficient queries on compressed bit arrays, SNARF does not adopt this approach. The additional space overhead incurred by rank-select structures contradicts SNARF's objective of optimizing for minimal space usage.

5.5.2 *Operation: Construction and Range Query*

Algorithm 27 gives the pseudo-code of how SNARF is constructed. For a given set of keys S and a bit array scaling factor K, the construction algorithm generates a model that represents the empirical cumulative distribution function (eCDF) of the keys, together with CBA. The process starts by training a model to approximate the

Algorithm 27 SNARF construction

```
Function BuildCDFModel(S)—builds the model to estimate the CDF of keys in set S
Function CompressPositions(posList)—encodes and compresses the numbers in set S
function CREATESNARF(S, K)
    MCDF ← BuildCDFModel(S)
    bitPositions ← EmptyList
    for each key in S do
        keyPos ← ⌊MCDF(key) × |S| × K⌋
        bitPositions.append(keyPos)
    end for
    compressedBits ← CompressPositions(bitPositions)
    return MCDF, compressedBits
end function
```

Algorithm 28 SNARF range query

```
Function IsBitInRange(a, b)—returns true if there is a 1 bit between range [a, b] else false
function ProcessRangeQuery(MCDF, K, n, CBA, L, R)
    lowBitPos ← ⌊mcdModel(L) × n × K⌋
    highBitPos ← ⌊mcdModel(R) × n × K⌋
    result ← CBA.IsBitInRange(lowBitPos, highBitPos)
    return result
end function
```

eCDF of the keys. The model then computes which bit positions should be set in the array. This bit array is subsequently compressed into the final CBA.

For a query with the range $[r, l]$, SNARF uses its learned CDF model to compute the mapped bit positions $f(l)$ and $f(r)$. Subsequently, if a 1 bit is detected within the corresponding range in CBA, it returns true, otherwise false as Algorithm 28 shows.

5.5.3 *Analysis: Space, Time and FPR*

In this part, we analyze the trade-off between the space utilization and the corresponding FPR of SNARF.

The focus lies on the space occupied by the CDF model and the CBA. The size of the CDF model is determined by the number of keys and the linear models employed. Assuming that each linear model uses two double-precision floating-point values, each model requires 128 bits. When storing keys as uint64 integers in the array, 64 bits are needed per key. Given that approximately $\frac{n}{1000}$ models are stored, the total space occupied by the models is around $\frac{192n}{1000}$ bits, which translates to approximately 0.2 bits per key.

Considering the sparse bit array, which requires nK bits, the CBA compressed using Golomb and Elias-Fano coding occupies no more than $2 + \log_2(K)$ bits per key. This is because the unary coding component of both Golomb and Elias-Fano schemes requires a maximum of $2n$ bits, while the binary representation part demands $\log_2(K)$ bits per key. Additionally, segmenting the CBA into blocks of βK bits introduces extra space overhead, approximately $\frac{nc}{\beta}$ bits, where c denotes the metadata size for each block.

In this section, we analyze the FPR of SNARF under both uniform and skewed workloads. The following terms and notation are used:

- z: Upper bound of the key range, where $z \gg nK$
- t: Number of linear model segments

For uniform point queries, there are z total queries, of which $z - n$ are negative. It is proved that SNARF returns false positives for approximately $\frac{z-n}{K}$ queries.

Dividing the key range into t segments $\Delta z_1, \Delta z_2, \ldots, \Delta z_t$ where $\sum_{i=1}^{t} \Delta z_i = z$, each segment $[z_{i-1}, z_i)$ contains $\frac{n}{t}$ keys. The number of negative queries in this segment is $z_i - z_{i-1} - \frac{n}{t}$. Keys in $[z_{i-1}, z_i)$ map to the bit array range $\left[(i-1)\frac{nK}{t}, i\frac{nK}{t}\right)$. Summing across all segments:

$$\sum_{i=1}^{t} \left(z_i - z_{i-1} - \frac{n}{t}\right) \times \frac{\frac{n}{t}}{\frac{nK}{t}} = \frac{1}{K} \sum_{i=1}^{t} \left(z_i - z_{i-1} - \frac{n}{t}\right) = \frac{z-n}{K}$$

Thus, the FPR is

$$FPR = \frac{\frac{z-n}{K}}{z-n} = \frac{1}{K}$$

Consider a range $[l, r]$ where $f(l-1) = f(r+1) = 0$ and $f(x) = 1$ for $x \in [l, r]$. If there are N keys contained in this query range, the number of false positive point queries is $r + 1 - l - N$.

For range queries of size R, the number of intersecting queries is $r + 1 + R - l$. At least $N + R$ of these are true positives. The upper bound on false positive range queries is

$$(r + 1 + R - l) - (N + R) = r + 1 - l - N$$

This equals the number of false positive point queries. Given the total false positive point queries are $\frac{z}{K}$ and negative range queries are at least $z - nR$, the FPR for range queries approximates

$$\frac{\frac{z}{K}}{z - nR} \approx \frac{1}{K} \text{(for small } R\text{)}$$

Assume queries follow a distribution $w(x)$ such that the probability within each segment $[z_{i-1}, z_i]$ is approximately uniform. From the uniform analysis, the FPR for each segment is $\frac{1}{K}$. Summing over all segments:

$$FPR = \sum_{i=1}^{t} (w(z_i) - w(z_{i-1})) \times \frac{\frac{n}{t}}{\frac{nK}{t}} = \frac{1}{K} \sum_{i=1}^{t} (w(z_i) - w(z_{i-1})) \approx \frac{1}{K}$$

Thus, under both uniform and skewed workloads, SNARF maintains a FPR of $\frac{1}{K}$ for point and small range queries.

5.6 Proteus

Proteus [6] introduces a novel self-designing approximate range filter that automatically optimizes its structure through data sampling. This autonomous configuration enables Proteus to minimize its FPR under strict space budgets, outperforming existing solutions. Prior approximate range emptiness (ARE) structures adopt one of two approaches: one is probabilistic AMQs (e.g., Prefix Bloom filters, Rosetta); the other is deterministic search trees (e.g., SuRF). Proteus advances the field by unifying these two design paradigms, enabling workload-adaptive configurations that dynamically balance probabilistic and deterministic filtering strategies for optimal performance.

The key innovation of Proteus resides in its contextual prefix false positive rate (CPFPR) model, a formal analytical construct that systematically captures FPR variations across the entire design landscape of prefix-based filters By rigorously quantifying these variations through probabilistic analysis, the CPFPR model provides the theoretical foundation for Proteus' adaptive optimization. This enables the filter to dynamically reconfigure its structure, achieving near-optimal FPR performance across diverse workloads and data distributions.

5.6.1 Structure: Trie and Prefix Bloom Filter

Proteus represents a hybrid filtering mechanism that incorporates both a trie with fixed depth l_1 and a prefix Bloom filter for prefix length l_2 ($l_1 < l_2$), serving as the respective representations of probabilistic and deterministic encodings for the key space. Figure 5.16 illustrates Proteus's encoding scheme for a 16-bit key space with an 8-depth trie and 12-bit Bloom filter prefixes.

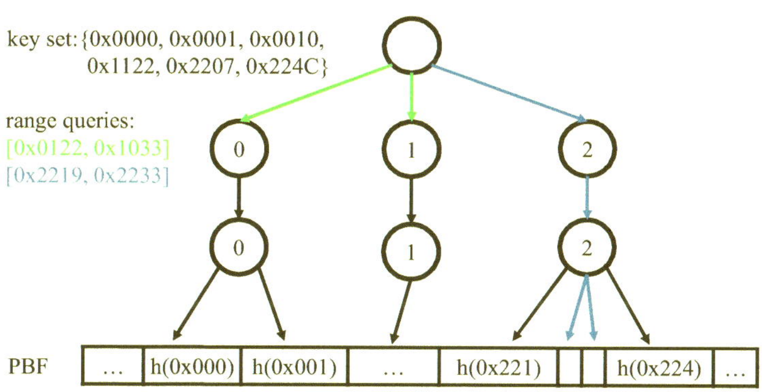

Fig. 5.16 An example of Proteus using 16-bit keys with a trie depth of 8 bits and a Bloom filter prefix length of 12 bits

The decision to utilize a uniform trie depth is twofold: it streamlines the modeling process and, crucially, it is a more efficient way of using memory. The fundamental principle is that in sparse regions of the key space, a coarse-grained encoding is more susceptible to false positives owing to the encoding of vast empty subspaces.

Conversely, applying coarse granularity encoding to densely populated key space areas typically results in smaller, less consequential empty subregions, thereby reducing the likelihood of false positives.

In contrast to SuRF, which inserts a unique prefix for each key, allowing for additional range counting and summation but limiting its performance under certain memory constraints, Proteus optimizes space constraints by adjusting trie depth and allocating the remaining space to the Bloom filter. Although Proteus is limited to empty range queries, this limitation can be mitigated by substituting the Bloom filter with a counting Bloom filter to enhance its functionality.

In general, Proteus combines the advantages of two encoding methods and compensates for their respective shortcomings. The Trie first filters out a substantial number of queries in constant time, whereas the prefix Bloom filter additionally addresses queries that reside in unpopulated subregions of the trie. Proteus allows for flexible allocation of resources based on context: it can allocate all resources to the trie or the entire set to the Bloom filter, essentially allocating corresponding prefix lengths to both.

5.6.2 Operation: Range Query

Proteus performs range queries by traversing the hybrid structure using a depth-first traversal. First, the trie is searched for corresponding prefixes. Should no matching leaf node be found in the trie, a result of negative will be returned to this query. If a leaf node is located, the search shifts to the Bloom filter for querying prefix extensions. An affirmative result from the Bloom filter leads the query to return positive. However, if all queries associated with the current leaf node in the Bloom filter yield negative results, the search resumes in the trie to locate the next matching node. The query returns negative when no further valid leaves exist in the trie and all queried Bloom filter regions have yielded negative results.

Taking the instance of Fig. 5.16, the query [0x0122,0x1033] illustrates the situation where no corresponding leaf is found in the trie; thus, the query returns negative. The query [0x2219, 0x2233] does find the corresponding leaf in the trie, yet no match results in the Bloom filter, leading to negative for the query.

5.6.3 Contextual Prefix False Positive Rate (CPFPR) Model

This section presents the contextual prefix false positive rate (CPFPR) model and provides the corresponding configuration algorithm.

The foundation for complex structures begins with formulating a single prefix Bloom filter for prefix with the length of l. The following terminology and notation are adopted:

- K: Dataset of keys.
- Q: An empty range query.
- X_i: Set of unique prefixes y with length i, where y is a prefix of some $x \in X$.
- LCP: Longest common prefix. For arbitrary sets X and Y, $\mathrm{lcp}(X, Y)$ denotes the longest LCP between $\{x, y | x \in X, y \in Y\}$.

For any empty range query Q, the prefix Bloom filter returns a false positive if any prefix in Q_l is positive (i.e., $Q_l \cap K_l \neq \emptyset$). The probability of this event is contingent on the proximity between Q and K, measured by $\mathrm{lcp}(Q, K)$. When $\mathrm{lcp}(Q, K)$ exceeds the key set's encoding prefix length, key and query elements become indistinguishable, leading to false positives. The range query FPR is expressed as Eq. 5.1, where p is the point query FPR:

$$P_{fp}(Q) = \begin{cases} 1 - (1-p)^{|Q_l|}, & \mathrm{lcp}(Q, K) < l \\ 1, & l \leq \mathrm{lcp}(Q, K) \end{cases} \tag{5.1}$$

Using a single prefix Bloom filter presents a trade-off between the number of query regions and the ability to distinguish queries near the key set, essentially a choice of prefix length. A plausible strategy to alleviate this challenge involves allocating memory across multiple Bloom filters. However, this approach has a notable drawback: each filter may only address a subset of queries. This limitation is justifiable if query patterns are highly heterogeneous, such that a unified prefix length fails to manage diverse query types. Yet, if the distribution splits into additional modes, the distinction between modes diminishes, making memory division into more filters increasingly less beneficial. Thus, given the marginal efficiency gains versus rising complexity, the analysis focuses on at most one additional Bloom filter.

Consider two Bloom filters for prefix lengths $l_1 < l_2$ with point query FPRs p_1 and p_2, respectively. Additional terminology includes:

- I_0, I_1: Indicator variables denoting whether intervals delimited by the first and last elements of Q_{l_1} are not entirely included in Q.
- I_2, I_3: Indicator variables denoting whether the first and last elements of Q_{l_1} are not in K_{l_2}. If $|Q_{l_1}| = 1$ and $Q_{l_1} \in K_{l_1}$, set $I_2 = 1$ and $I_3 = 0$.
- L, R: Collections of l_2 prefixes that intersect Q, each encompassing the first and last prefixes of Q_{l_1}, respectively.
- $P_{l_1}(i)$: Probability that i of the l_1 prefixes fully within Q return false positives, expressed as the binomial probability mass function with $n = |Q_{l_1}| - I_0 - I_1$ and $p = p_1$ (Eq. 5.3).
- $\bar{P}_L, \bar{P}_R$: Probabilities that L or R are unresolved by the first filter and return only negatives in the second.

Similar to the single filter case, $l_1 < l_2 \leq \text{lcp}(Q, R)$ leads to false positives, so consider $\text{lcp}(Q, R) < l_2$. For any Q, each prefix in Q_{l_1} fully contained in Q either yields a false positive or true negative. A false positive requires performing $2^{l_2-l_1}$ queries on the second filter. Notably, Q_{l_1} shares at most two common prefixes with K (at query ends), which may yield false or true positives. These end prefixes, potentially the only ones not fully in Q, lead to variable second-filter queries. Equation 5.2 addresses end prefix cases:

$$\bar{p_L} = p_1^{I_2} \cdot I_0 (1 - p_2)^{|L|}, \bar{p_R} = p_1^{I_3} \cdot I_1 (1 - p_2)^{|R|} \tag{5.2}$$

For remaining false positive combinations requiring $2^{l_2-l_1}$ second-filter queries:

$$P_{l_1}(i) = \binom{|Q_{l_1}| - I_0 - I_1}{i} p_1^i (1 - p_1)^{|Q_{l_1}|-I_0-I_1-i} \tag{5.3}$$

Thus, the range query FPR is

$$P_{fp}(Q) = 1 - \bar{p_L} - \bar{p_R} - \sum_{i=0}^{|Q_{l_1}|-I_0-I_1} P_{l_1}(i) \left((1 - p_2)^{i2^{l_2-l_1}}\right) \tag{5.4}$$

Increasing the number of filters does not eliminate the probabilistic nature of Bloom filters. If l_1 and l_2 differ significantly, the second filter's probability of capturing ranges missed by the first is extremely low. Allocating more memory to the first filter reduces false positives but diminishes its capacity to handle relevant queries, as the second filter's memory is constrained.

Replacing the first Bloom filter with a uniform-depth trie forms the Proteus structure. Due to the trie's deterministic nature, only prefixes matching leaf nodes are directed to the Bloom filter. Similarly, only the first and last members of Q_{l_1} can match the key set, so at most $2^{l_2-l_1+1} - 2$ prefixes are queried at l_2. The FPR is

$$P_{fp}(Q) = \begin{cases} 0, & \text{lcp}(Q, K) < l_1 < l_2 \\ 1 - (1 - p)^{I_2|L|+I_3|R|}, & l_1 \leq \text{lcp}(Q, K) < l_2 \\ 1, & l_1 < l_2 \leq \text{lcp}(Q, K) \end{cases} \tag{5.5}$$

Compared to Eq. 5.4, Eq. 5.5 exhibits a more concise structure, facilitating easier modeling. When the second Bloom filter consumes the same memory, Proteus demonstrates superior FPR performance. However, this introduces a fixed memory constraint at l_1, where the selection of l_1 directly affects the subsequent memory allocation for the Bloom filter. Thus, the subsequent focus is on how to select prefix lengths l_1 and l_2 to achieve optimal FPR.

Algorithm 29 illustrates how Proteus determines prefix lengths by calculating and comparing the expected FPR for each configuration and then selecting the

Algorithm 29 Prefix length selection modeling process

```
Input k—The Binary size of maximum key length
Input m—The Binary size of memory budget
Input S—Empty sample queries set
Output (l1, l2)—Prefix lengths for optimal FPR
Function trieMem(l)—Returns the size of trie memory at depth l
Function BFfpr(m, n)—Returns Bloom filter FPR for m bits and n elements
function SelectOptimalPrefixes(K, k, m, S)
    unsigned int trieResolvedCount[k]
    map regionCountMatrix[k][k]
    for each Q in S do
        minLen ← lcp(K, Q)
        for tLen from 0 until trieMem(tLen) ≤ m do
            if tLen > minLen then
                trieResolvedCount[tLen] += 1
            end if
            for bLen from tLen+1 to k do
                if tLen < minLen && bLen > minLen then
                    regionCountMatrix[tLen][bLen].add(I2|L| + I3|R|)
                end if
            end for
        end for
    end for
    minFPR ← 1
    for tLen from 0 until trieMem(tLen) ≤ m do
        tFPR ← 1—(trieResolvedCount[tLen] / |S|)
        if tFPR ≤ minFPR then
            minFPR ← tFPR
            (l1, l2) ← (tLen, 0)
        end if
        for bLen from tLen+1 to k do
            bFPR ← BFfpr(m—trieMem(tLen), |K_bLen|)
            totalFPR ← 0
            processedQueries ← trieResolvedCount
            for each (regionCount, freq) in regionCountMatrix[tLen][bLen] do
                totalFPR ← totalFPR + regionCount × bFPR × freq
                processedQueries ← processedQueries + freq
            end for
            totalFPR ← totalFPR + (|S| − processedQueries) / |S|
            if minFPR ≥ totalFPR then
                minFPR ← totalFPR
                (l1, l2) ← (tLen, bLen)
            end if
        end for
    end for
    return (l1, l2)
end function
```

one with the lowest FPR. This process involves extracting and retaining critical information from the set of empty sample queries and key set to compute Eq. 5.5:

- **Bloom Filter FPR**: $p = \left(1 - e^{-ln(2)}\right)^{\lceil m/n \cdot ln(2) \rceil}$, where n is numbers of key prefixes and m is the allocated bit count.
- **Key Prefix Statistics**: Since Bloom filter's FPR depends on element count, the number of unique key prefixes in K_l is essential. This is computed by calculating successive LCPs of the sorted key set, an $O(|K|)$ operation.
- **Trie Memory Estimation**: K_l is used to estimate trie size at each depth l, based on LOUDS-Sparse and LOUDS-Dense implementations in SuRF.
- **Query Prefix Processing**: For any $Q \in S$, the corresponding trie depth (obtained via $lcp(Q, K)$, requiring search for the nearest K member to Q) and the number of regions covering Q (determined by shifting Q's bounds to each prefix length and computing differences) are needed.

With the above information, Eq. 5.5 is computed for each configuration, and results are averaged to find the expected FPR. The key advantage of pre-gathering all information is the ability to batch-process FPR for queries sharing the same Q_l at a given prefix length. However, when range query sizes vary significantly, most queries have unique prefix counts, potentially leading to $O(|S|)$ calculations per configuration.

To reduce computational overhead, query prefix counts are binned into k exponentially increasing bins (k = maximum key length in bits). Bin i includes queries with prefix counts in $[2^{i-1}, 2^i - 1]$ and their average count; bin 0 handles queries resolved in the trie. Each non-empty bin undergoes a single batch FPR calculation using the average prefix count, limiting calculations to at most k batches per configuration. This significantly reduces modeling workload with minimal accuracy loss, as the probability of a negative response for empty queries decreases exponentially with the number of prefix queries.

5.7 Summary and Comparison

5.7.1 Summary of Range Filters

- **Adaptive Range Filter** (ARF). As a prefix-based range filter, ARF arranges in a binary tree structure, converting escalation and de-escalation operations into leaf node splitting and merging using a clock method. Its tree structure achieves logarithmic time complexity for query operations.
- **Succinct Range Filter** (SuRF). As a prefix-based range filter, SuRF takes advantage of FST and LOUDS-DS to construct itself, which is more effective in FPR and space-consuming than basic trie or binary trees. This architecture achieves logarithmic time complexity for query operations.
- **Robust Space-Time Optimized Range Filter** (Rosetta). As a hash-based range filter, Rosetta constructs itself using stacked Bloom filters. This design decreases the FPR when facing correlated queries.
- **Bloom Range Filter** (BloomRF). As a hash-based range filter, BloomRF uses PMHF to build itself. It tackles the issue of not preserving order in basic hashing.

Table 5.2 Comparison of range filters

Filter	Type	Construction latency	Query latency	FPR
ARF	Prefix-based	High	High	High
SuRF	Prefix-based	High	Medium	High
Rosetta	Hash-based	Medium	Medium	Low
BloomRF	Hash-based	Medium	Medium	Medium
SNARF	Learned-based	Low	Low	Medium
Proteus	Hybrid	High	Medium	Low

- **Sparse Numerical Array-Based Range Filters** (SNARF). As a learned-enhanced range filter, SNARF organizes itself using linear model and encoding approaches. By introducing these scheme, SNARF achieves constant-time complexity build time and logarithmic time complexity for query operations.
- **Proteus**. As a hybrid range filter, Proteus combines FST and prefix Bloom Filter together. This design takes the advantages of prefix- and hash-based range filters.

5.7.2 Comparison of Range Filters

Table 5.2 compares six range filters in construction latency, query latency, and false positive rate (FPR). Among prefix-based range filters, SuRF achieves superior space efficiency and lower false positive rates (FPR) compared to ARF by utilizing LOUDS-DS-encoded FSTs. Regarding hash-based range filters, Rosetta and BloomRF exhibit distinct trade-offs: Rosetta employs a stacked Bloom filter design that preserves key suffixes, resulting in lower FPR for correlated queries but longer query latency. In contrast, BloomRF leverages piecewise-monotone hash functions (PMHF) to ensure locality-preserving hash values for similar prefixes, improving query speed at the cost of higher FPR for correlated queries. For learned-based range filters, SNARF utilizes simple linear models, enabling faster construction and lower FPR for non-correlated queries relative to other filters. As for hybrid range filters, Proteus combines FSTs with prefix Bloom filters to capitalize on their complementary strengths, achieving consistently low FPR across both large and small ranges. However, the computational overhead of its CPFPR model leads to a prolonged construction time.

5.7.3 Conclusion

Different types of range filters exhibit distinct trade-offs in construction time, query latency, and false positive rate (FPR). Selecting an appropriate range filter tailored to specific applications and dataset workloads can maximize retrieval efficiency for relevant systems and applications.

References

1. Alexiou, K., Kossmann, D., Larson, P.Å.: Adaptive range filters for cold data: Avoiding trips to siberia. Proc. VLDB Endow. 1714–1725 (2013). https://doi.org/10.14778/2556549.2556556
2. Zhang, H., Lim H., Leis, V., et al.: Surf: Practical range query filtering with fast succinct tries. In: Proceedings of ACM SIGMOD International Conference on Management of Data, pp. 323–336 (2018). https://doi.org/10.1145/3183713.3196931
3. Luo, S., Chatterjee, S., Ketsetsidis, R., et al.: Rosetta: a robust space-time optimized range filter for key-value stores. In: Proceedings of ACM SIGMOD International Conference on Management of Data, pp. 2071–2086 (2020). https://doi.org/10.1145/3318464.3389731
4. Mößner, B., Riegger, C., Bernhardt, A., et al.: bloomRF: on performing range-queries in Bloom-Filters with piecewise-monotone hash functions and prefix hashing. In: Proceedings of ACM EDBT International Conference on Extending Database Technology, pp. 131–143 (2022). https://doi.org/10.48550/arXiv.2207.04789
5. Vaidya, K., Chatterjee, S., Knorr E., et al.: SNARF: a learning-enhanced range filter. In: Proceedings of the VLDB Endowment, pp. 1632–1644 (2022). https://doi.org/10.14778/3529337.3529347
6. Knorr, E.R., Lemaire, B., Lim A., et al.: Proteus: a self-designing range filter. In: Proceedings of ACM SIGMOD International Conference on Management of Data, pp. 1670–1684 (2022). https://doi.org/10.1145/3514221.3526167